Exploring maths

Home Book

PEARSON
Longman

Anita Straker, Tony Fisher, Rosalyn Hyde,
Sue Jennings and Jonathan Longstaffe

6

Published and distributed by Pearson Education Limited, Edinburgh Gate, Harlow, Essex, CM20 2JE, England
www.longman.co.uk

First published 2009

ISBN-13 978-1-405-84424-6

Typeset by Tech-Set, Gateshead

Printed and bound in Great Britain at Scotprint, Haddington

The publisher's policy is to use paper manufactured from sustainable forests.

Picture credits

The publisher would like to thank the following for their kind permission to reproduce their photographs:

(Key: b-bottom; c-centre; l-left; r-right; t-top)

Alamy Images: Victor De Jesus 16; Design Pics Inc 107c; Kathy deWitt 122; Chris Howes/Wild Places Photography 34t; Matthew Jackson 99; Chris Pearsall 14t; Janine Wiedel Photolibrary 31; **Corbis:** Robert Michael 59b; **DK Images:** Demetrio Carrasco(c)Rough Guides 1; Peter Gardner 12br; Steve Gorton 14b; Dave King 9; Matthew Ward 12bl; **Getty Images:** Dag Sundberg/The Image Bank 107r; **iStockphoto:** 34b, 65b, 78, 106; Mike Bentley 65t; Rob Broek 90; Anthony Brown 80; Russell Du parcq 68; Jeremy Edwards 13; Peter Genis 85; Christine Glade 17; Joanne Green 58, 110; Stefan Hermans 96; Dietmar Klement 56; David Lewis 43; Maciej Noskowski 11; Steve Pepple 60; Thomas Perkins 98; Owen Price 72; Stephen Rees 12bc; Alexander Sakhatovsky 55t; Willi Schmitz 55b; Laszlo Sovany 103t; Christian Wheatley 104; Yong Hian Lim 109; Lisa F. Young 46; **Nature Picture Library:** Sue Flood 107l; **PA Photos:** AP Photo/Keystone, Arno Balzarini 67; **Pearson Education Ltd:** Merrill Education 3; Prentice Hall, Inc 22; **Photolibrary. com:** Index Stock Imagery 59t; Stockbyte 12t; **Science Photo Library Ltd:** WORLDSAT INTERNATIONAL INC. 70; **Texas Instruments:** Suzie Williams Photography 33

Cover images: *Front:* **Corbis:** Gianni Dagli Orti

All other images © Pearson Education

Picture Research by: Louise Edgeworth

Acknowledgements

We are grateful to the following for permission to reproduce copyright material:

David Blatner for a screenshot from www.joyofpi.com, granted with kind permission; and Albert Washuettl, Friends of Pi Club for a screenshot of http://www.wasi.org/PI/pi_club.html, granted with kind permission.

Every effort has been made to trace the copyright holders and we apologise in advance for any unintentional omissions. We would be pleased to insert the appropriate acknowledgement in any subsequent edition of this publication.

Contents

Tier 6

Powers and roots

 Did you know that...?

A googol is 10^{100}, or 1 with one hundred zeros after it.

This was the answer to the million pound question on the television programme *Who wants to be a millionaire?* when the contestant who won was suspected of cheating by getting signals from friends in the audience.

TASK 1: Squares, cubes and roots

 Points to remember

⊙ $\sqrt{n}$ is the **square root** of n.
   The square root can be positive or negative.
⊙ $\sqrt[3]{n}$ is the **cube root** of n.
   The cube root of a positive number is positive, and of a negative number is negative.
⊙ You can estimate square roots and cube roots using **trial and improvement**.

(1) Solve these equations by using trial and improvement.
   Make a table to help you.
   Give your answers correct to one decimal place.

   a $a^3 = 45$ b $a(a + 4) = 40$

(2) The cube of 17 is 4913.

   When you add the digits of this cube together the sum is 17, the number itself.

   $$17^3 = 4913 \qquad 4 + 9 + 1 + 3 = 17$$

   The number 1 has this property since $1^3 = 1$ and the sum of the digits of 1 is 1.

   What other numbers less than 50 have this property?

TASK 2: Equivalent calculations using powers of 10

 Points to remember

- When you multiply, or divide, both numerator and denominator of a calculation by the same number, the answer does not change.
- If you multiply the numerator by a number, the answer is multiplied by the same number.
  For example: $\frac{3.8}{0.2} = 19$, $\frac{3.8 \times 10}{0.2} = 19 \times 10 = 190$
- If you divide the numerator by a number, the answer is divided by the number.
  For example: $\frac{3.8}{0.2} = 19$, $\frac{3.8 \div 10}{0.2} = 19 \div 10 = 1.9$
- If you multiply the denominator by a number, the answer is divided by the same number.
  For example: $\frac{3.8}{0.2} = 19$, $\frac{3.8}{0.2 \times 10} = \frac{3.8 \div 10}{0.2 \times 10 \div 10} = \frac{3.8 \div 10}{0.2} = 19 \div 10 = 1.9$
- If you divide the denominator by a number, the answer is multiplied by the same number.
  For example: $\frac{3.8}{0.2} = 19$, $\frac{3.8}{0.2 \div 10} = \frac{3.8 \times 10}{0.2 \div 10 \times 10} = \frac{3.8 \times 10}{0.2} = 19 \times 10 = 190$

Do these questions **without using a calculator**. Show your working.

1. Given that $2.8 \times 6.4 = 17.92$, work out:

    a 28×64　　　　b 2.8×640　　　　c 28×0.64　　　　d 0.028×0.64

2. Given that $15.2 \div 4.75 = 3.2$, work out:

    a $15.2 \div 47.5$　　　b $1.52 \div 4.75$　　　c $152 \div 4.75$　　　d $1.52 \div 0.475$

3. Given that $26 \times 32 = 832$, work out:

    a 0.26×0.32　　　b $832 \div 2.6$　　　c $8.32 \div 0.32$　　　d $83.2 \div 0.032$

4. Given that $\frac{4.5 \times 17.2}{1.2} = 64.5$, work out:

    a $\frac{45 \times 172}{12}$　　b $\frac{0.45 \times 1.72}{0.12}$　　c $\frac{4500 \times 1.72}{120}$　　d $\frac{450 \times 0.172}{0.012}$

TASK 3: Standard form

Points to remember

⊙ To **multiply** two numbers in index form, add the indices, so $a^m \times a^n = a^{m+n}$.

⊙ To **divide** two numbers in index form, subtract the indices, so $a^m \div a^n = a^{m-n}$.

⊙ A number in **standard form** is of the form $A \times 10^n$, where $1 \leqslant A < 10$ and n is an integer.

The key for entering numbers in standard form is usually [EXP] or [^].
Use the negative key [−] or the sign change key [+/−] for negative powers.

Example 1

To enter 3.75×10^4, press:

[3] [·] [7] [5] [EXP] [4]

or:

[3] [·] [7] [5] [×] [1] [0] [^] [4]

Example 2

To enter 2.8×10^{-3}, press:

[2] [·] [8] [EXP] [+/−] [3]

or:

[2] [·] [8] [×] [1] [0] [^] [+/−] [3]

---

1. Write in standard form:
   a 73 000 000
   b 0.000 84
   c 422 000
   d 93 300
   e 0.000 000 81
   f 52 321
   g 0.009 35
   h 0.000 000 6

2. Write as ordinary numbers. Use your calculator.
   a 5.9×10^4
   b 5.36×10^{-3}
   c 9.4×10^3
   d 6.68×10^{-2}
   e 9×10^9
   f 5.82×10^{-4}
   g 5.2×10^6
   h 7.03×10^{-1}

3. Write in standard form:
   a 58×10^3
   b 27.8×10^{-5}
   c 0.77×10^{-3}
   d 48×10^{-4}

Expressions and formulae

TASK 1: Algebraic fractions

> **Points to remember**
> - You can only add and subtract fractions with the same denominator.
> - The rules for adding and subtracting algebraic fractions are the same as for numerical fractions.
> - To add or subtract fractions with different denominators first convert them to the same denominator.
> - You can simplify a fraction by dividing the numerator and denominator by common factors.

1 Simplify these expressions.

a $\dfrac{11}{b} - \dfrac{3}{b}$

b $\dfrac{10}{ab} + \dfrac{25}{ab}$

c $\dfrac{34}{xy} - \dfrac{7}{xy}$

2 Simplify these expressions.

a $\dfrac{8}{a} + \dfrac{7}{b}$

b $\dfrac{16}{c} + \dfrac{9}{d}$

c $\dfrac{11}{a} - \dfrac{5}{b}$

d $\dfrac{3}{c} - \dfrac{6}{d}$

e $\dfrac{12}{xy} + \dfrac{21}{wz}$

f $\dfrac{13}{pq} - \dfrac{8}{rs}$

3 Simplify these expressions by dividing the numerator and denominator by common factors.

a $\dfrac{39}{65}$

b $\dfrac{96}{144}$

c $\dfrac{27a}{33b}$

d $\dfrac{11a}{25a}$

e $\dfrac{6ab}{9ac}$

f $\dfrac{15ad}{19a^2c}$

g $\dfrac{28xy}{49xz}$

h $\dfrac{36x^2}{27xy}$

i $\dfrac{a^3bc^2}{ab^3c}$

TASK 2: Linear equations

Points to remember

⊙ You can use inverse operations to solve simple **linear equations**.

⊙ If there are brackets, multiply them out first.

⊙ If the unknown letter is on both sides of the equation, rearrange the equation so the unknown letter is on one side only.

⊙ If there are fractions, multiply through by the lowest common denominator.

1. Find the value of x.

   a $8x + 26 = 98$ b $7x - 18 = 59$
   c $6x + 29 = 8x + 13$ d $10x - 7 = 7x + 5$

2. Find the value of x.

   a $4(9 + 5x) = 116$ b $7(6 + 10x) = 462$
   c $8(3x + 7) + 5(4x + 8) = 316$ d $3(7x + 8) + 6(4x + 9) = 213$

3. Find the value of x.

   a $\frac{x}{7} + 41 = 44$ b $\frac{x}{6} + 53 = 58$
   c $\frac{1}{7}(2x - 3) = 5$ d $\frac{1}{8}(x + 12) = 3$
   e $\frac{2}{3}x + 5 = \frac{1}{3}x + 14$ f $\frac{4}{5}x + 9 = \frac{2}{5}x + 25$

TASK 3: Expanding brackets

Points to remember

⊙ Writing $6(9x + 3)$ as $54x + 18$ is called **expanding the brackets** or **multiplying out the brackets**.

⊙ Each term inside the bracket is multiplied by the number or letter outside, e.g. $4(a + 7) = 4a + 28$ or $a(a + 5) = a^2 + 5a$.

⊙ The product of two expressions is normally written without the $\times$ sign, e.g. as $(a + 5)(a + 7)$.

⊙ To expand a pair of brackets, each term in the first bracket is multiplied by each term in the second bracket, e.g. $(a + 3)(a + 5) = a^2 + 3a + 5a + 15 = a^2 + 8a + 15$

You can use a multiplication grid to help you to expand brackets.

×	b	+	2	
7	$7b$	+	14	$7b + 14$

×	a	+	3	
a	a^2	+	$3a$	$a^2 + 3a$
$+$				$+$
5	$5a$	+	15	$5a + 15$
				$a^2 + 8a + 15$

1. Multiply out the brackets.

   a $3(x + 5)$

   b $8(y - 2)$

   c $9(x + 7)$

   d $5(6x - 1)$

   e $8(8a + 9b)$

   f $2(7p - 4q + 2r)$

2. Multiply out and simplify.

   a $6(x + 7) + 3(x + 9)$

   b $2(y + 5) + 7(y + 8)$

   c $4(x + 5) + 10(x + 1)$

   d $5(p + 11) + 3(p + 9)$

   e $6(13a + 8) + 9(3a - 2)$

   f $8(6x - 3) + 7(2x + 7)$

3. Use a multiplication grid to expand the brackets.

   a $(x + 7)(x + 9)$

   b $(y + 4)(y + 5)$

   c $(x + 8)(x + 1)$

   d $(p + 6)(p + 5)$

   e $(a + 11)(a + 3)$

   f $(x + 9)^2$

TASK 4: Factorising expressions

⊙ Points to remember

- ⊙ A factor of an algebraic expression divides exactly into each term of the expression.
- ⊙ You can take a common factor of each term of an expression outside a bracket, e.g. $6b + 10ab = 2b(3 + 5a)$, because $2b$ is a factor of $6b$ and a factor of $10ab$.
- ⊙ A quadratic expression can be written as the product of two linear expressions, e.g. $a^2 + 3a + 1 = (a + 2)(a + 1)$.

1. Factorise these expressions by taking out common factors.

   a $6x + 4$

   b $20y - 35$

   c $3a^2 + 15a$

   d $14b^2 - 2b$

   e $25pq + 5qr$

   f $p^2qr - pq^2r + pqr^2$

(2) Find the matching pairs.

A $(a + 2)(a + 6)$

B $a^2 + 8a + 16$

C $a^2 + 8a + 15$

D $(a + 3)(a + 5)$

E $a^2 + 8a + 12$

F $(a + 1)(a + 7)$

G $(a + 4)(a + 4)$

H $a^2 + 8a + 7$

(3) Factorise these expressions.

a $a^2 + 10a + 21$ b $a^2 + 9a + 20$ c $a^2 + 12a + 11$

TASK 5: Identities

⊙ Points to remember

⊙ When two algebraic expressions can be expanded to produce exactly the same combination of terms they are said to be **identical**.

⊙ The sign ≡ means **identically equal to**.

(1) Use the diagram on the right to prove that:
$$(x + 6)(x + 10) \equiv x^2 + 16x + 60$$

a Write an expression for the area of the rectangle.

b Write an expression for the sum of the four shapes inside the rectangle and simplify your answer.

c Explain why the two expressions are equal.

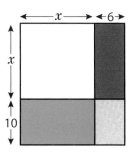

(2) The identity $x^2 - y^2 = (x - y)(x + y)$ is called the **difference of two squares**. Use the identity to calculate these differences.

a $9^2 - 4^2$ b $12^2 - 8^2$ c $19^2 - 9^2$

d $25^2 - 5^2$ e $14^2 - 6^2$ f $34^2 - 26^2$

TASK 6: Changing the subject of a formula

Points to remember

⊙ A **formula** is a way of expressing a relationship using symbols.
⊙ When a formula is written as $d = st$, then d is the **subject** of the formula.
⊙ You can rearrange a formula to make a different letter the subject, for example $s = \dfrac{d}{t}$ or $t = \dfrac{d}{s}$.

1 Which of these cards match the formula $l = m + n$?

A $m = n - l$

B $n = l - m$

C $m = l + n$

D $n = l + m$

E $m = l - n$

F $n = m - l$

2 Make the letter in brackets the subject of each formula.

a $A = lw$ (w)

b $P = 2(l + w)$ (w)

c $m = lr + n$ (r)

d $a = bc + d$ (d)

e $q = ax - y$ (x)

f $q = ax - y$ (y)

g $S = \dfrac{PR}{a}$ (R)

h $S = \dfrac{PR}{a}$ (a)

i $V = \pi r^2 h$ (h)

j $V = \pi r^2 h$ (r)

Proportional reasoning

TASK 1: Fraction calculations

⊙ **Points to remember**

- ⊙ To add and subtract fractions, change them to the same denominator.
- ⊙ If there are whole numbers, deal with them first.
- ⊙ To multiply fractions, cancel, then multiply the numerators and multiply the denominators.
- ⊙ To divide fractions, turn the divisor upside down and multiply by it.
- ⊙ To multiply or divide mixed numbers, first change them to improper fractions.

① Work out each of these. Simplify your answer where possible.

a $2\frac{1}{4} + 3\frac{2}{5}$ b $1\frac{3}{8} + 2\frac{2}{3}$ c $2\frac{5}{8} - 1\frac{5}{12}$ d $3\frac{5}{12} - 1\frac{3}{4}$

② Work out each of these. Cancel before multiplying where possible.

a $\frac{1}{6} \times \frac{3}{8}$ b $\frac{2}{3} \times \frac{3}{4}$ c $1\frac{3}{7} \times 4\frac{1}{5}$ d $2\frac{3}{8} \times 1\frac{3}{5}$

③ Work out each of these. Cancel before multiplying where possible.

a $\frac{1}{4} \div \frac{1}{3}$ b $\frac{3}{16} \div \frac{9}{14}$ c $2\frac{5}{8} \div 4\frac{2}{3}$ d $3\frac{3}{5} \div 2\frac{2}{5}$

④ a A jar of sugar has $3\frac{3}{5}$ cupfuls of sugar in it. A cake recipe uses $\frac{3}{10}$ of a cupful of sugar. How many cakes can be made from the sugar in the jar?

b A jug of cream is two thirds full. The chef uses four fifths of the cream in the jug to make the cake. How full is the jug of cream now?

TASK 2: Reciprocals

> ### ● Points to remember
> - The **reciprocal** of a is $1 \div a$.
> - The reciprocal of $\frac{a}{b}$ is $\frac{b}{a}$.
> - The reciprocal of a^n is a^{-n} for any power n.

(1) Find the reciprocal of each of these numbers.

     a 500   **b** 0.008   **c** 90   **d** 0.625

(2)   **a** Write as a decimal the reciprocal of each of the integers from 21 to 29.

     b Which of the integers have reciprocals that are recurring decimals?

(3) **Without using a calculator**, arrange these in order, smallest first.
Show your working.

$$\frac{1}{8} \qquad \frac{2}{15} \qquad \frac{3}{25} \qquad \frac{4}{31} \qquad \frac{5}{34}$$

TASK 3: Percentage increases and decreases

> ### ● Points to remember
> - Percentage increases and decreases can be calculated using **decimal multipliers**.
> - **Simple interest** is paid on the original investment.
>   The same amount of interest is paid each year.
> - **Compound interest** is paid on the original investment plus any previous interest. The amount of interest paid increases each year.

Where appropriate, give your answers correct to the nearest penny.

1. How much will you have in the bank if you invest at these annual rates of compound interest?
   a £900 at 3% for 4 years
   b £3000 at 4.5% for 7 years

2. £1250 is invested at 6% per annum simple interest.
   Work out the total amount in the account after 3 years.

3. Shares in the stock market can go down in value as well as up.
   How much would your shares be worth if you had invested as follows?
   a £10 000, which lost 12% each year for 3 years
   b £750, which gained 5% each year for 5 years

4. The price of a new television is £423.
   Each year, its value falls by 12% of its value at the start of the year.
   Work out the value of the television at the end of 2 years.

TASK 4: Reverse percentages

⊙ Points to remember

- ⊙ The **unitary method** involves finding the size of one part as an intermediate step.
- ⊙ Percentage increases and decreases, and **reverse percentages**, can be calculated using the unitary method or by using **decimal multipliers**.

1. A pair of shoes was originally priced at £60.
   In a sale, the shoes are reduced to £36.
   What is the percentage reduction in the price of the shoes?

2. In a sale, all the prices are reduced by 25%.
   The sale price of some jeans is £30.
   What was the price of the jeans before the sale?

3. After a 10% price increase, a dishwasher costs £374.
   How much was the dishwasher before the increase?

4. After dieting, David weighed 76 kg.
   This was a 5% loss in his weight.
   How much did David weigh before his diet?

(5) A silver bangle is on sale at £96.
This is 60% of its original price.
What was the original price?

(6) A house cost £150 000 in 1995.
By 2009, its value had increased by 230%.
How much did the house cost in 2009?

(7) James and Joanna paid £123 500 for their house.
This was 5% less than the asking price.
What was the asking price?

(8) The value of a car goes down by 10% each year.
Jack buys a car.
After one year the car has a value of £2700.
Work out the original value of the car.

TASK 5: Rate, speed and density

Points to remember

⊙ A **compound measure** involves more than one unit. Examples are:
average speed $= \dfrac{\text{distance}}{\text{time}}$ and density $= \dfrac{\text{mass}}{\text{volume}}$

⊙ **Per** in a measure such as miles per hour means 'for every'.

⊙ These diagrams for speed, distance and time and density, mass and volume can help you to solve problems.

$$\triangle \begin{array}{c} D \\ \hline S \mid T \end{array} \qquad \triangle \begin{array}{c} M \\ \hline D \mid V \end{array}$$

1. Lucy cycles 8.4 km in 18 minutes.
   Work out her average speed.

2. Leroy drives 208 km at an average speed of 64 km/h.
   In hours and minutes, how long does his does his journey take?

3. A hiker walks for $3\frac{1}{2}$ hours at an average speed of $2\frac{1}{2}$ mph.
   How many miles did he walk?

4. The mass of 40 cm³ of aluminium is 104 g.
   Calculate the density of aluminium.

5. The density of lead is 11 g/cm³.
   A bucket made of lead uses 160 cm³ of lead.
   Work out the mass of the bucket.

6. The density of cork is 0.2 g/cm³.
   Find the volume of a cork float with a mass of 180 g.

7. Jamina drove for 2 hours at an average speed of 40 km/h.
   She then drove for 3 hours at an average speed of 50 km/h.
   What was her average speed for the whole journey?

TASK 6: Proportionality

● Points to remember

⊙ a and b are **directly proportional** if their ratio $a : b$ stays the same as a and b increase or decrease:
$\frac{a}{b} = k$, where k is constant

⊙ a and b are **inversely proportional** if a increases as b decreases at the same rate:
$ab = k$, where k is constant

⊙ When you solve problems involving direct or inverse proportion:
   – use the unitary method;
   – make sure that corresponding quantities are in the same units;
   – ask yourself whether the answer should be larger or smaller.

1. In 2008, £1 could be exchanged for 1.68 euros. How many euros did you get for £150?

2. Eight identical stamps cost £2.56. What is the cost of five of the stamps?

3　50 litres of petrol costs £48.
How much will 20 litres of petrol cost?

4　Sam takes 20 minutes to drive from home to work at an average speed of 30 mph.

How long would it take him if he drove at an average speed of 40 mph?

5　Three men build a driveway in 6 days.
How long would two men take?

6　A workman earns £45 for 4 hours' work.
How much does he earn in 10 hours?

7　In a week, the grass on my lawn grew 28 mm.
On average, how much did it grow in 4 days?

8　Six hikers on Exmoor have enough food to last them 2 days.
How many days would the same food last four hikers?

Enquiry 1

TASK 1: Representative samples

> **⦿ Points to remember**
>
> ⦿ The whole set of people or items that might be part of a study is called a **population**.
>
> ⦿ A **sample** is used when it would be too difficult to study every person or item in the population.
>
> ⦿ A **representative sample** represents a population fairly. It is not biased towards any group in the population.
>
> ⦿ In a **random sample** each person or item has an equal chance of being chosen. A random sample may not be representative.

① The table shows the school roll at an 11–16 school.

Year	7	8	9	10	11
Boys	106	111	106	108	104
Girls	95	102	108	96	99

The school is planning to survey a sample of its pupils on attitudes to smoking.

Comment on each of these methods of sampling.

⦿ **Method 1**

Tina visits Year 7 classes each morning for a week and surveys five boys and five girls.

⦿ **Method 2**

Robert uses an alphabetical list of all 1000 pupils in the school and selects every 20th pupil.

⦿ **Method 3**

Sunil makes a random selection of 5% of the boys and 5% of the girls from each year.

② Some pupils at a school are selected at random.
They complete a questionnaire about homework.

Why might conclusions based on the completed questionnaires **not** be valid?

③ Tina wants to find out about the distances that pupils live from her school.

The school has about 2000 pupils. Tina decides to base her findings on a sample of about 100 pupils.

a What does Tina have to do to make her findings a valid representation of the whole school?

b Write a list of **all** the things that Tina needs to do to select her sample.

TASK 2: Frequency polygons

◉ Points to remember

⊙ A **frequency polygon** is a statistical diagram used to represent discrete or continuous grouped data. It shows the shape of a distribution more clearly than a frequency diagram drawn with bars.

⊙ To draw a frequency polygon:
  – plot the frequencies against the midpoints of the class intervals;
  – join the points with straight lines.

You will need some graph paper.

① Two representative samples of pupils estimate the size of an angle.
The first sample consists of 25 Year 7 pupils and the second of 25 Year 10 pupils.
Their estimates are shown in this grouped frequency table.

Estimated angle (a, degrees)	Year 7	Year 10
$10 \leqslant a < 20$	2	0
$20 \leqslant a < 30$	2	1
$30 \leqslant a < 40$	6	8
$40 \leqslant a < 50$	11	14
$50 \leqslant a < 60$	3	2
$60 \leqslant a < 70$	1	0

Draw two frequency polygons, one for each set of data.

(2) Rob works at a garden centre.

Rob grows some plants from seed.
He measures the heights of a sample of the plants.
His results are shown in this frequency polygon.

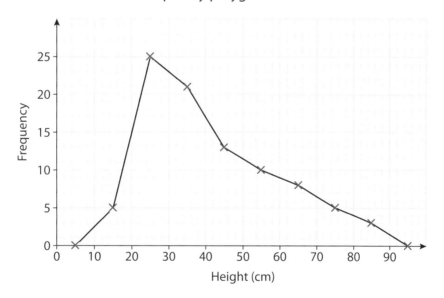

a How many plants are included in Rob's sample?

b How many of the plants are between 40 cm and 60 cm?

c How many of the plants are less than 30 cm?

d One of the seeds was selected at random.
What is the probability that this seed grows to a plant greater than 50 cm in height?

TASK 3: Average and range of grouped data 1

Points to remember

- The **modal class** of a set of grouped data is the class interval with the greatest frequency.
- To calculate an estimate of the **mean** of a set of grouped data, work out:

$$\frac{\text{the sum of (midpoints of class intervals} \times \text{frequency)}}{\text{the sum of the frequencies}}$$

1 This grouped frequency table represents the time, t, that 25 pupils take to complete five press-ups.

a Write down the modal class for this set of data.

b Estimate the mean of this set of data.

Time (t, seconds)	Frequency
$0 \leqslant t < 10$	3
$10 \leqslant t < 20$	7
$20 \leqslant t < 30$	10
$30 \leqslant t < 40$	4
$40 \leqslant t < 50$	1

2 25 pupils were asked to estimate the length of the road outside their school in metres.

The results are shown in this frequency polygon.

a Write down the modal class for this set of data.

b Estimate the mean.

3 This grouped frequency table shows the time taken for 100 pupils to travel to school.

a Draw a frequency polygon to represent this data.

b What is the modal class?

c Calculate an estimate of the mean.

Time (t, minutes)	Frequency
$0 \leqslant t < 5$	2
$5 \leqslant t < 10$	14
$10 \leqslant t < 15$	28
$15 \leqslant t < 20$	35
$20 \leqslant t < 25$	20
$25 \leqslant t < 30$	1

TASK 4: Average and range of grouped data 2

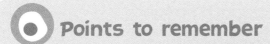

Points to remember

⊙ For a set of grouped data, **the estimated range** is:

maximum possible value − minimum possible value

The maximum possible value is the highest value in the highest class interval. The minimum possible value is the lowest interval in the lowest class interval.

⊙ To **estimate the median**, assume that the data is evenly spread throughout the class interval in which the median occurs.

Estimate the range and median for the sets of data given in questions 1, 2 and 3 in Task 3.

TASK 5: Comparing sets of grouped data

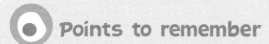

Points to remember

⊙ You can compare two or more sets of grouped data by comparing:
- **average** values (the modal class or the estimated mean or median);
- the **spread** of values (the estimated range);
- the **shapes** of frequency polygons.

⊙ Statistical investigations are based on the data handling cycle.

You will need some graph paper.

1. Two representative samples of pupils from Years 7 and 10 estimated the size of an angle. Their estimates are shown in the grouped frequency table below.

In Task 2, question 1, you drew a frequency polygon for each set of data on **different** grids.

a Now use graph paper to draw a frequency polygon for each set of data on the **same** grid.

b In which year group do the angle estimates vary the least? Explain your answer.

Estimated angle (a, degrees)	Year 7	Year 10
$10 \leqslant a < 20$	2	0
$20 \leqslant a < 30$	2	1
$30 \leqslant a < 40$	6	8
$40 \leqslant a < 50$	11	14
$50 \leqslant a < 60$	3	2
$60 \leqslant a < 70$	1	0

2. This grouped frequency table represents the times, t, that 25 pupils and 25 adults took to complete five press-ups.

Time (t, seconds)	Frequency	
	Pupils	Adults
$0 \leqslant t < 10$	3	8
$10 \leqslant t < 20$	7	15
$20 \leqslant t < 30$	10	2
$30 \leqslant t < 40$	4	0
$40 \leqslant t < 50$	1	0

a Use graph paper to draw a frequency polygon for each set of data on the same grid.

b Compare the averages and range of these sets of data.

3. Sadaf is planning a statistical investigation. She is going to compare the reaction times of pupils of different ages in her school. She makes a list of tasks that she has to do but they are not in order.

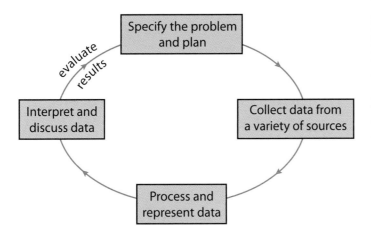

Write some instructions to do a reaction test.

Do the test and record the reaction times.

Decide when I will collect the data.

Decide how I am going to sample.

Put the data in a table.

Draw frequency diagrams.

Work out averages.

Write a hypothesis.

Draw a conclusion about my hypothesis.

Decide who will be in my sample.

Decide how many will be in my sample.

Write down what I notice about my graphs.

Design a data collection sheet.

Rewrite Sadaf's list under each of the headings in the data handling cycle. Add to the list if you think she has missed anything out.

TASK 6: Scatter graphs and lines of best fit

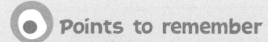

Points to remember

⊙ A **scatter graph** is used to show whether there is a relationship between two variables.

⊙ A **line of best fit** is a straight line that represents the best estimate of the relationship between the two variables on a scatter graph.

⊙ To draw the line of best fit, draw a straight line so that there are roughly equal numbers of points of the scatter graph on each side of it.

You will need some graph paper.

1 *2001 level 7*

The scatter diagram shows the mass of goldcrests at different times during winter days. It also shows the line of best fit.

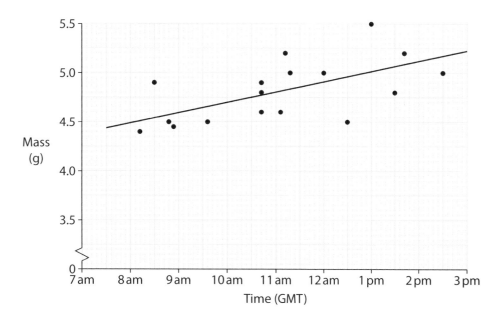

a Estimate the mass of a goldcrest at 11:30 am.

b Estimate how many grams, on average, the mass of a goldcrest increases during 1 hour.

c Write the coordinates (time, mass) of the point that represents the goldcrest least likely to survive the night if it is cold. Explain why you chose that point.

2 A survey is carried out to compare the ages of people with their reaction times in a test.

Age (years)	Reaction time (seconds)
45	0.15
62	0.31
83	0.58
24	0.20
76	0.62
63	0.43
44	0.21
42	0.25
37	0.18
50	0.49

a Plot the data on a scatter graph. Use the x-axis for the range of ages, from 0 to 90 years, and the y-axis for reaction times, from 0 to 1 seconds.

b Draw a line of best fit.

c Use your line of best fit to estimate the reaction time of a 30-year-old.

Geometrical reasoning

TASK 1: Isosceles triangle problems

> ### ⊙ Points to remember
>
> ⊙ In a regular polygon with n sides:
> - the **exterior angle** is $\frac{360}{n}$;
> - the **interior angle** is $180 -$ exterior angle;
> - there are n identical isosceles triangles;
> - the **angle at the centre** is $\frac{360}{n}$.
>
> ⊙ Triangles formed by a chord and two radii of a circle are isosceles.

1. A, B and C are vertices of a regular octagon with centre O.

   a Calculate angle OAB.
   Show your working.

   b Calculate angle OAC.
   Show your working.

2. A, B and C are points on the circumference of a circle with centre O.

   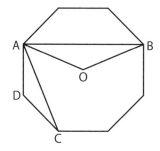

   AOC is a diameter of the circle.

   a Explain why triangles OAB and OBC are isosceles.

   b When angle $x = 76°$:

   i Show that angle $y = 38°$.
   Explain your method clearly. Give a reason for each step.

   ii Work out angle OBC.
   Explain your method clearly. Give a reason for each step.

   c Show that angle ABC = 90°.

   d When angle $y = 30°$, show that triangle OBC is equilateral.

TASK 2: Evidence or proof?

Points to remember

⊙ The angles in geometrical shapes are often connected by simple rules.

⊙ A **proof** is a logical, step-by-step procedure with reasons and explanations given for each step.

⊙ A proof shows that a rule works for all values.

⊙ You can **demonstrate** that a rule works by testing it with particular values.

① In the diagram, BC is parallel to DE. ABD and ACE are straight lines that intersect at A.
AB = BC

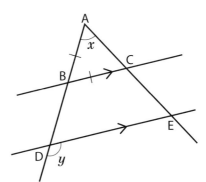

a Show that when angle x is 40°, angle y is 80°.
Explain your method clearly.
Give a reason for each step.

b Prove that angle $y = 2 \times$ angle x.

② ABC is an isosceles triangle.
D is a point on AB produced.

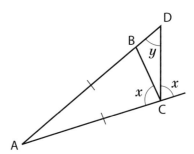

a Show that when angle x is 70°, angle y is 30°.
Explain your method clearly.
Give a reason for each step.

b Prove that angle $y = 3 \times$ angle $x - 180$.

c Explain why angle x is more than 60°.

TASK 3: Congruent triangles

1. These triangles are not drawn to scale.

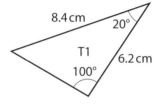
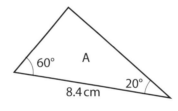
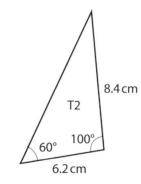
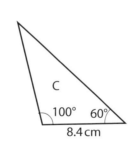
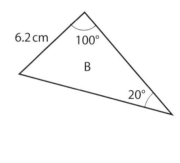

  a Explain why triangle A is congruent to triangle T1.

  b Is triangle B or triangle C congruent to triangle T2?
     Give a reason for your answer.

2. ABCD is a rhombus.
   Its diagonals intersect at O.

   Prove that triangle ABD is congruent
   to triangle CBD.

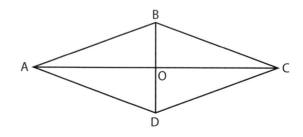

3 ABCDE is a regular pentagon.

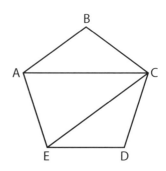

   a Prove that triangle ABC is congruent to triangle CDE.

   b What does this tell you about triangle ACE?

TASK 4: Radii, chords and tangents

 Points to remember

- The tangent at a point on a circle is **perpendicular to the radius** at the point.
- The tangents to a circle from a point outside the circle are **equal in length**.
- The perpendicular from the centre of a circle to a chord **bisects the chord**.
- The line joining the midpoint of a chord to the centre of the circle is **perpendicular to the chord**.

1 Each diagram shows a circle with centre O. A, B and C are points on the circumference.

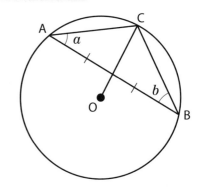

   a **i** Which line in the diagram is a chord?

      ii Angle ACO = 60°

         Work out angle a and angle b.
         Show your working, giving reasons.

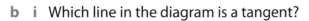

   b **i** Which line in the diagram is a tangent?

      ii Angle AOB = 140°

         Work out angle c and angle d.
         Show your working, giving reasons.

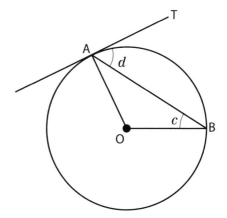

2 Each diagram shows a circle, centre O. A, B and C are points on the circumference. PA is a tangent to the circle at A.

Find the size of each of the angles marked with a letter x. (not drawn accurately) Give reasons for your answers.

a

b

c

d

e

f

TASK 5: Similar shapes

Points to remember

When two shapes are **similar**:

⊙ each shape is an **enlargement** of the other;

⊙ **corresponding sides** are in the same ratio, so they are connected by a scale factor;

⊙ angles at **corresponding** vertices are equal.

1 Explain why these rectangles are similar.

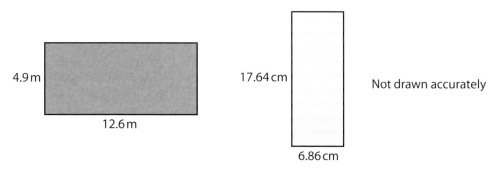

4.9 m

12.6 m

17.64 cm

6.86 cm

Not drawn accurately

② In these triangles, the angles marked x are equal and the angles marked y are equal.

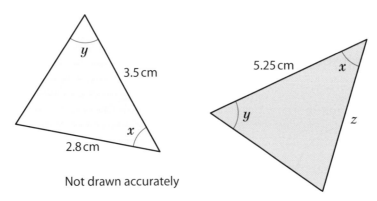

Not drawn accurately

a Explain why the triangles are similar.

b Work out the length marked z.

③ The diagram shows a shaded triangle labelled T and a set of triangles labelled A to F.

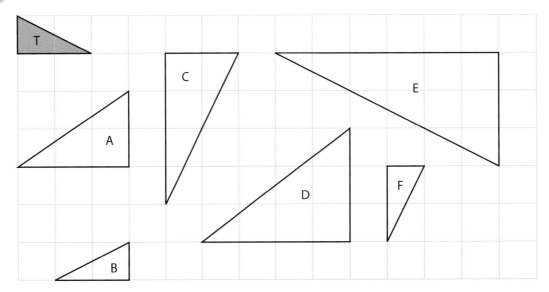

a Which of these right-angled triangles are congruent to triangle T?

b Which of these right-angled triangles are similar to triangle T?

④ These shapes are similar.

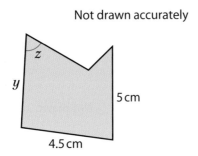

Not drawn accurately

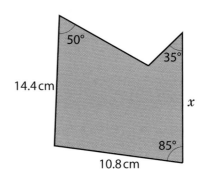

a Write down the size of angle z.

b Show that x is double y.

TASK 6: Investigating properties of shapes

 Points to remember

- ⊙ You can use properties of angles and shapes to solve geometrical problems.
- ⊙ You can solve multi-step problems by making decisions and explaining your reasoning.

Draw a large circle on a piece of A4 scrap paper. You could draw round a plate or bowl.

Follow the instructions below carefully. As you do this make a list of the names of the shapes you create and identify the parts of shapes that you are using, for example a chord or arc of a circle.

Make a truncated tetrahedron

1 Fold your circle in half exactly and then in half again. Open it out.

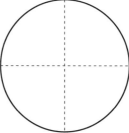

2 Fold in one of the curved edges so it just meets the centre of the circle.

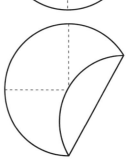

3 Fold in another curved part in the same way.

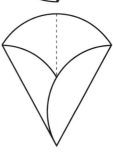

4 Fold in the final curved part to touch the centre and to make an equilateral triangle.

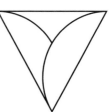

5 Fold a vertex of the equilateral triangle down to meet the midpoint of the opposite side.

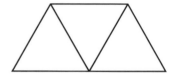

6 Fold the left and right triangles over onto the central triangle to make a smaller equilateral triangle. If you open the triangles up again the three vertices will come together to form a tetrahedron.

7 Open the tetrahedron out again to the equilateral triangle. Fold each of the three vertices to meet at the centre to form a hexagon.

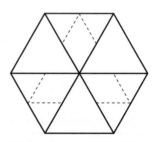

8 Open the triangles out again and then tuck one of the vertices inside the 'pocket' in the adjacent vertex. Tuck the final vertex in to form a **truncated tetrahedron**.

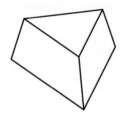

Linear graphs and inequalities

TASK 1: Sketching and drawing linear graphs

Points to remember

- The **normal form** of a linear equation is $y = ax + b$.
- The graph of the equation $y = ax + b$ has **gradient** a and **intercept** on the y-axis at $(0, b)$.
- When you **sketch** a linear graph, label the axes and mark the origin and the intercept on the y-axis.
- To make an **accurate drawing** of a linear graph, calculate the coordinates of three points, plot them and draw a line through them using a ruler and sharp pencil.

You need some graph paper, a ruler and pencil.

1. Write the gradient and intercept for the graphs of these equations.
   Sketch the graphs.
   Use a new grid for each graph.

   a $y = x + 14$ b $y = x - 9$

   c $y = 4x - 2$ d $y = 2x + 11$

   e $y = -2x$ f $y = -0.5x + 3$

2. Rearrange these equations into their normal form, and write the gradient and intercept.
   Sketch the graphs.
   Use a new grid for each graph.

   a $y - x = 10$ b $y + x = 7$

3. On graph paper, make an accurate drawing of the graph of $y - 2x = 5$.

TASK 2: Graphs of inverse functions

> ## Points to remember
> ⊙ An **inverse function** does the reverse of a function.
> ⊙ When you **reflect** the graph of a function in the line $y = x$ you get the graph of the inverse function.

(1) Sketch the graphs of the function and its inverse.
Use a different grid for each pair of graphs.
Label the lines with their equations.

a $x \rightarrow \boxed{+12} \rightarrow x + 12$

b $x \rightarrow \boxed{\times 5} \rightarrow 5x$

c $x \rightarrow \boxed{\div 2} \rightarrow \dfrac{x}{2}$

d $x \rightarrow \boxed{+2.5} \rightarrow x + 2.5$

e $x \rightarrow \boxed{-5.5} \rightarrow x - 5.5$

f $x \rightarrow \boxed{\div 5} \rightarrow \dfrac{x}{5}$

(2) Work out the inverse functions for these functions.

a $x \rightarrow \boxed{\times 2} \rightarrow \boxed{+1} \rightarrow 2x + 1$

b $x \rightarrow \boxed{+3} \rightarrow \boxed{\times 8} \rightarrow 8(x + 3)$

c $x \rightarrow \boxed{\times 4} \rightarrow \boxed{-3} \rightarrow 4x - 3$

d $x \rightarrow \boxed{-5} \rightarrow \boxed{\times 6} \rightarrow 6(x - 5)$

e $x \rightarrow \boxed{+7} \rightarrow \boxed{\div 6} \rightarrow \dfrac{x + 7}{6}$

f $x \rightarrow \boxed{\div 4} \rightarrow \boxed{+1} \rightarrow \dfrac{x}{4} + 1$

(3) Sketch the graphs of the function and its inverse.
Use a different grid for each pair of graphs. Label each line with its equation.

a $x \rightarrow \boxed{\times 2} \rightarrow \boxed{+5} \rightarrow 2x + 5$

b $x \rightarrow \boxed{\times 4} \rightarrow \boxed{-5} \rightarrow 4x - 5$

c $x \rightarrow \boxed{+3} \rightarrow \boxed{\times 7} \rightarrow 7(x + 3)$

d $x \rightarrow \boxed{-4} \rightarrow \boxed{\times 4} \rightarrow 4(x - 4)$

TASK 3: Properties of linear graphs

 Points to remember

- Graphs of **parallel** lines have the same gradient.
- When the equation of a line is written in the form $y = ax + b$, the value of a will be the same for any pair of parallel lines.
- The gradient of a line **perpendicular** to $y = ax + b$ is $-\frac{1}{a}$.
- The equation of any line perpendicular to $y = ax + b$ is $y = -\frac{1}{a}x + c$.

1. a What is the gradient of the line $y = 8x + 4$?

    b A line is parallel to $y = 3x + 1$. It intersects the y-axis at $(0, -3)$.
       What is its equation?

    c A line is parallel to $y = -5x - 2$. It intersects the y-axis at $(0, 14)$.
       What is its equation?

    d A line is parallel to the line passing through $(1, 2)$ and $(2, 8)$.
       It intersects the y-axis at $(0, 3)$.
       What is its equation?

2. A line has equation $y = 2x - 1$.
    What are the equations of the lines parallel to this line that pass through these points?

    a $(1, 6)$ b $(5, 5)$ c $(3, 6)$

3. For each question decide whether the lines AB and CD are parallel, perpendicular or neither.

    a A $(-1, 1)$ B $(0, 5)$ and C $(0, 1)$ D $(1, 5)$

    b A $(0, 2)$ B $(2, 8)$ and C $(-3, 7)$ D $(3, 5)$

    c A $(-1, 7)$ B $(1, 1)$ and C $(-1, 1)$ D $(1, 7)$

    d A $(-6, 6)$ B $(6, 4)$ and C $(0, 1)$ D $(1, 7)$

    e A $(0, 3)$ B $(4, 5)$ and C $(-4, 5)$ D $(0, 7)$

    f A $(-5, 8)$ B $(-1, 0)$ and C $(0, 3)$ D $(6, 0)$

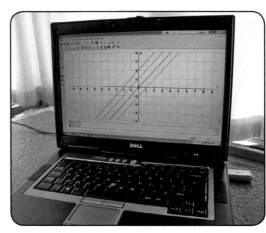

TASK 4: Solving simultaneous equations 1

 Points to remember

⊙ Two different non-parallel linear graphs intersect at one unique point.

⊙ Two linear equations are **simultaneously equal** at the point of intersection of their graphs.

⊙ Problems with two unknowns that are represented by two linear equations can be solved by finding the point of intersection of their graphs.

⊙ Two linear equations whose graphs are parallel have **no solutions**.

You will need graph paper for these tasks.

1. Solve these pairs of simultaneous equations by drawing accurate graphs. Check your answers by substituting the values of x and y back into the equations.

   a $3x + 2y = 17$ .... (1)
   $4x - 5y = 15$ .... (2)

   b $5x - 2y = 2$ .... (1)
   $4x + y = 12$ .... (2)

   c $2x + 3y = 25$ .... (1)
   $3x + y = 13$ .... (2)

   d $2x + 5y = 11$ .... (1)
   $4x - 3y = 9$ .... (2)

2. For each problem set up two equations. Draw their graphs and solve the problem.

   a Shula and Leila are buying lunch.

   Shula pays £21 for 6 sandwiches and 4 coffees.
   Leila pays £13 for 4 sandwiches and 2 coffees.

   Work out the cost of:
   i one sandwich
   ii one coffee

   b Kiri and Malak are buying tickets for a boat ride.

   Kiri pays £75 for 5 adult and 7 child tickets.
   Malak pays £54 for 3 adult and 6 child tickets.

   Work out the cost of:
   i an adult's ticket
   ii a child's ticket

TASK 5: Solving simultaneous equations 2

 Points to remember

- You can use **substitution** to solve a pair of simultaneous equations in x and y:
  - rearrange one equation to make y the subject;
  - substitute for y in the second equation, which gives the value of x;
  - substitute the value for x into either equation to find the value for y.

- You can use **elimination** to solve a pair of simultaneous equations in x and y:
  - when the coefficient of one of the variables is the same for both equations, subtract the equations, which will give the value of one variable;
  - substitute this value into either equation to find the value of the other variable.

- You can multiply every term in an equation by the same number to change the coefficients of the variables.

1. Use the **method of substitution** to solve these simultaneous linear equations.

   a $y = 3x - 7$ .... (1)
      $4x + 3y = 18$ .... (2)

   b $x = 4y - 17$ .... (1)
      $3x + 2y = 47$ .... (2)

   c $x - y = 2$ .... (1)
      $2x + 3y = 19$ .... (2)

   d $x + 4y = 18$ .... (1)
      $5x + 3y = 22$ .... (2)

   e $x = 5y + 1$ .... (1)
      $3x - 4y = 14$ .... (2)

   f $y = x - 7$ .... (1)
      $3x + 5y = 37$ .... (2)

2. Use the **method of elimination** to solve these simultaneous linear equations.

   a $4x + 7y = 23$ .... (1)
      $4x + 2y = 18$ .... (2)

   b $5x + 2y = 25$ .... (1)
      $x + 2y = 13$ .... (2)

   c $7x + 5y = 9$ .... (1)
      $7x + 2y = 12$ .... (2)

   d $9x + 3y = 27$ .... (1)
      $4x + 3y = 7$ .... (2)

   e $3x + 5y = 17$ .... (1)
      $6x + 2y = 14$ .... (2)

   f $2x + 4y = 12$ .... (1)
      $3x + 11y = 24$ .... (2)

TASK 6: Solving linear inequalities

Points to remember

⊙ A statement using one of the four symbols $<$, $>$, $\leq$ or $\geq$ is an **inequality**.

⊙ $x < 3$ means that x is any number that is **less than** 3.
$x > 5$ means that x is any number that is **greater than** 5.
$x \leq 10$ means that x is any number that is **less than or equal to** 10.
$x \geq 0$ means that x is any number that is **greater than or equal to** zero.

⊙ Solutions of linear inequalities can be shown on a number line, e.g.

$x < 3$

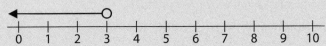

$x \geq 5$

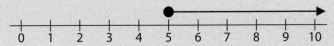

---

(1) Represent each of these inequalities on a number line from −5 to 5.

   a $x < 5$ 　　　　 **b** $x \geq 1$ 　　　　 **c** $x \leq 2$ 　　　　 **d** $x > -2$

   e $x < -3$ 　　　　 **f** $-5 < x < 5$ 　　　 **g** $0 \leq x \leq 4$ 　　 **h** $-4 < x < -3$

(2) Write the inequality that describes the region shown in each diagram.

(3) List all the whole numbers which satisfy these inequalities.

   a $2 \leq x < 7$ 　　　　　 **b** $8 < x < 14$ 　　　　 **c** $15 < x \leq 20$

   d $55 \leq x \leq 60$ 　　　 **e** $10 < x < 15$ 　　　 **f** $100 \leq x < 103$

Trigonometry 1

TASK 1: Pythagoras' theorem

  Points to remember

- In a right-angled triangle, the **hypotenuse** is opposite the right angle and is the longest side.

- **Pythagoras' theorem** shows that in a right-angled triangle the area of the square on the hypotenuse is equal to the sum of the areas of the squares on the other two sides, or $a^2 + b^2 = c^2$.

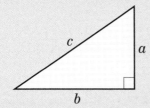

- **Pythagorean triples** are sets of three integers that satisfy the relationship $a^2 + b^2 = c^2$: for example, 3, 4, 5 or 5, 12, 13.

- You can use Pythagoras' theorem to check whether a triangle has a right angle or not.

① Sunil draws this right-angled triangle accurately.
He draws a square on the hypotenuse of the triangle.

   a On which side of the triangle does Sunil draw the square?

   b Work out the area of the square that Sunil draws.

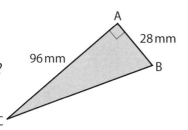

② The diagram shows a sketch of a triangle.

Jane says:

'The triangle has a right angle at B.'

Explain how Jane can check whether her statement
is true or false without drawing the triangle.

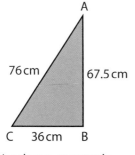

Not drawn accurately

③ Peter's teacher tells him that a 3, 4, 5 triangle has a right angle.
Peter decides that a 4, 5, 6 triangle must also have a right angle.
Use Pythagoras' theorem to show that Peter is wrong.

④ Which of these triangles is the odd one out? Explain why.

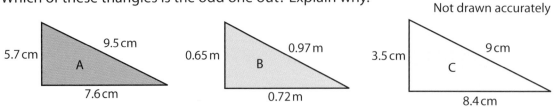

Not drawn accurately

TASK 2: Introducing trigonometry

Points to remember

⊙ The **hypotenuse** is the side opposite the right angle.

⊙ The **opposite side** is opposite the marked angle.

⊙ The **adjacent side** is between the marked angle and the right angle.

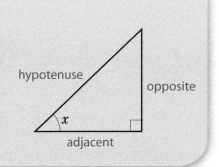

① Sketch the triangles below.
Label the hypotenuse, opposite and adjacent sides in each triangle.

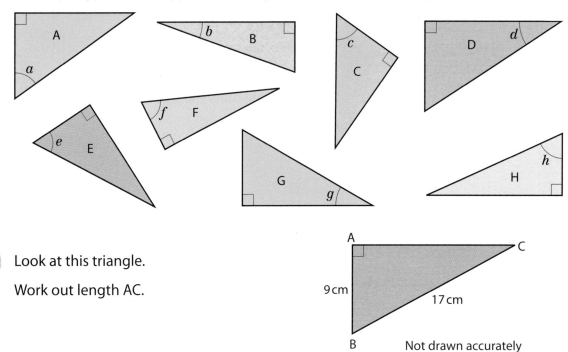

② Look at this triangle.

Work out length AC.

TASK 3: Using the tangent ratio

Points to remember

⊙ You can use the **tangent** ratio to find unknown lengths of shorter sides in right-angled triangles.

⊙ $\tan x = \dfrac{\text{opposite}}{\text{adjacent}}$

Example

Work out the length y.

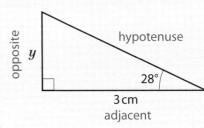

$\tan = \dfrac{\text{opposite}}{\text{adjacent}}$

$\tan 28° = \dfrac{y}{3}$

$0.532 = \dfrac{y}{3}$

$y = 3 \times 0.532 = 1.60 \text{ cm to 2 d.p.}$

You will need a scientific calculator.

Give all your answers to three significant figures.

1 Find the lengths a, b and c.
You will need to make a sketch of the triangles. Remember to show your working.

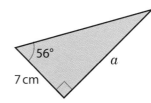
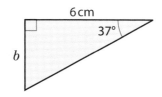
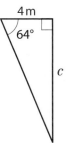

Not drawn accurately

2 Find the lengths e, f and g.
You will need to make a sketch of the triangles. Remember to show your working.

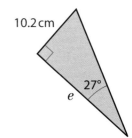
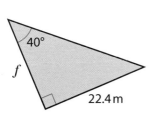
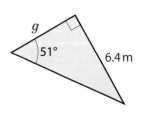

Not drawn accurately

TASK 4: Using sine and cosine ratios

 Points to remember

⊙ Use the **sine**, **cosine** and **tangent** ratios to find unknown lengths in right-angled triangles.

⊙ Choose the right ratio to use to solve each problem.

$$\sin x = \frac{\text{opposite}}{\text{hypotenuse}} \qquad \cos x = \frac{\text{adjacent}}{\text{hypotenuse}} \qquad \tan x = \frac{\text{opposite}}{\text{adjacent}}$$

Example

a Work out the length y.

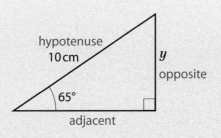

$$\sin = \frac{\text{opposite}}{\text{hypotenuse}}$$

$$\sin 65° = \frac{y}{10}$$

$$0.906 = \frac{y}{10}$$

$$y = 9.06 \text{ cm}$$

b Work out the length z.

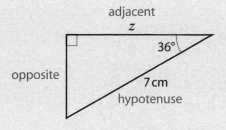

$$\cos = \frac{\text{adjacent}}{\text{hypotenuse}}$$

$$\cos 36° = \frac{z}{7}$$

$$0.809 = \frac{z}{7}$$

$$z = 5.66 \text{ cm}$$

c Work out the length x.

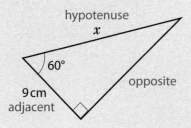

$$\cos = \frac{\text{adjacent}}{\text{hypotenuse}}$$

$$\cos 60° = \frac{9}{x}$$

$$0.500 = \frac{9}{x}$$

$$x = \frac{9}{0.5} = 18 \text{ cm}$$

You will need a scientific calculator.
Write all your answers to two decimal places.

1 Find the lengths a, b, c and d.
You will need to make a sketch of the triangles.
Remember to show your working.

Use the sine ratio for a and b.

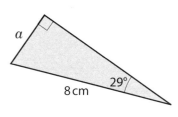

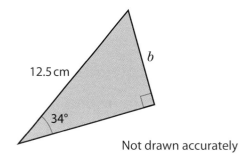

Not drawn accurately

Use the cosine ratio for c and d.

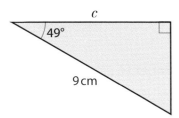

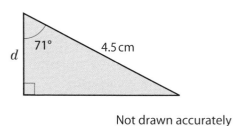

Not drawn accurately

2 Find the lengths e and f.
You will need to make a sketch of the triangles.
Remember to show your working.

Use the sine ratio for e.   Use the cosine ratio for f.

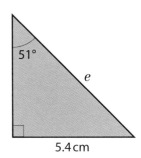

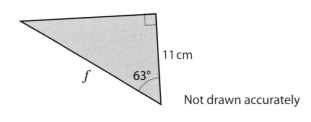

Not drawn accurately

Expressions, equations and graphs

TASK 1: Simultaneous equations 1

 Points to remember

⊙ A pair of **simultaneous linear equations** has a solution at the point where their graphs intersect.

⊙ A pair of equations whose graphs are parallel has no solution.

⊙ When one variable is given in terms of the other you can use the **method of substitution** to solve the equations.

⊙ When one variable is not given in terms of the other you can use the **method of elimination** to solve the equations.

⊙ Multiply every term in an equation by the same number to change the coefficients of the variables.

① For each pair of equations say whether they have one solution for x and y or no solution. Find the solution if it exists.

    a $2x + y = 7$ .... (1)
       $3x - y = 3$ .... (2)

    b $3x + 5y = 8$ .... (1)
       $3x + 5y = -4$ .... (2)

    c $x - 3y = 5$ .... (1)
       $4x - 12y = 27$ .... (2)

    d $3x + y = 7$ .... (1)
       $10x - 2y = 2$ .... (2)

② Solve these pairs of simultaneous linear equations using the method of elimination.

    a $4x + 2y = 18$ .... (1)
       $2x + 5y = 29$ .... (2)

    b $3x + 4y = 7$ .... (1)
       $7x + 3y = 29$ .... (2)

    c $3x + 4y = 32$ .... (1)
       $2x + 3y = 23$ .... (2)

    d $9x + 2y = 32$ .... (1)
       $5x + 4y = 38$ .... (2)

    e $7x + 2y = 52$ .... (1)
       $2x + 5y = 37$ .... (2)

    f $6x + 5y = 34$ .... (1)
       $7x + 9y = 65$ .... (2)

TASK 2: Simultaneous equations 2

Points to remember

- Look carefully at pairs of equations to decide which method to use.
- If one variable is given in terms of the other, use **substitution**.
- Otherwise, use **elimination**. Make the number part of the coefficients of one of the variables the same by multiplying each equation by a suitable scale factor.
  - If the signs of the coefficients are both the same, subtract the equations.
  - If the signs of the coefficients are different, add the equations.
- You can check your answer by drawing a graph.

1. Solve these pairs of simultaneous linear equations using the method of elimination.

a $6x + 5y = 27$ .... (1)
$3x + 2y = 12$ .... (2)

b $7x + 2y = 13$ .... (1)
$15x - 4y = 3$ .... (2)

c $2x - y = 8$ .... (1)
$5x - 3y = 18$ .... (2)

d $4x - 3y = 22$ .... (1)
$7x - 9y = 31$ .... (2)

e $2x + 9y = 27$ .... (1)
$5x - 3y = 42$ .... (2)

f $2x - 3y = 12$ .... (1)
$3x - 4y = 17$ .... (2)

g $5x + 8y = 28$ .... (1)
$3x - 11y = 1$ .... (2)

h $2x - y = 13$ .... (1)
$3x - 3y = 15$ .... (2)

TASK 3: Expanding brackets 1

 Points to remember

⊙ To expand $2x(3x + 4)$ multiply every term inside the bracket by $2x$ to get $6x^2 + 8x$.

⊙ To expand $(x + 3)(x + 5)$ multiply every term in the first bracket by every term in the second bracket to get $x^2 + 3x + 5x + 15 = x^2 + 8x + 15$.

⊙ You can use a multiplication grid to help you expand brackets, e.g.

$(a + 2)(a + 4) = a^2 + 2a + 4a + 8$
$= a^2 + 6a + 8$

×	a	+	4	
a	a^2	+	$4a$	$a^2 + 4a$
+				+
2	$2a$	+	8	$2a + 8$
				$a^2 + 6a + 8$

⊙ Use 'First Outside Inside Last' (**FOIL**) to remember how to expand brackets.

1 Expand the brackets and then simplify the expressions.

    a $5(a + 8) + 20$ **b** $7(x + 7) + 9x$ **c** $6(b + 3) - 5(b + 2)$

    d $19p - 12(p + 5)$ **e** $4(3a + 7) + 7(a - 3)$ **f** $6(5x - 4) + 8(3x - 5)$

    g $3(6x + 9) + x - 20$ **h** $4(b + 7) + 5(2b - 3)$

2 Expand the brackets.

    a $(x + 6)(x + 4)$ **b** $(x + 7)(x + 3)$ **c** $(x + 7)^2$

    d $(x + 3)(x + 8)$ **e** $(x + 6)(x + 9)$ **f** $(x + 5)(x + 10)$

    g $(x + 9)(x + 8)$ **h** $(x + 11)(x + 7)$ **i** $(x + 15)^2$

TASK 4: Expanding brackets 2

 Points to remember

⊙ You can use a multiplication grid to help you expand brackets.

⊙ Use 'First Outside Inside Last' (**FOIL**) to remember how to expand brackets.

$(a + 2)(a + 4) = a^2 + 4a + 2a + 8$
$= a^2 + 6a + 8$

1 Expand the brackets.

    a $(x - 6)(x + 4)$ **b** $(x - 6)(x - 4)$ **c** $(x - 7)(x + 7)$

    d $(x - 3)(x - 8)$ **e** $(x - 6)(x + 9)$ **f** $(x + 5)(x - 10)$

    g $(x - 9)(x - 8)$ **h** $(x - 11)(x + 7)$ **i** $(x - 15)(x + 15)$

TASK 5: Factorising quadratic expressions

> ### ◉ Points to remember
>
> ◉ The reverse of expanding brackets is **factorising**.
> ◉ To factorise a quadratic expression find two linear expressions that are factors, e.g.
> $$x^2 + x - 6 = (x + 3)(x - 2)$$
> ◉ To work out the factors of $x^2 + x - 6$:
>   – as the coefficient of x^2 is 1, each bracket begins with x, i.e. $(x\quad)(x\quad)$;
>   – as the sign in front of 6 is $-$, the brackets must be $(x +\quad)(x -\quad)$;
>   – find a factor pair of -6 whose sum is $+1$: $(x + 3)(x - 2)$.

1 Factorise these quadratic expressions.

    a $x^2 + 9x + 14$ **b** $x^2 - 5x - 14$ **c** $x^2 + 5x - 14$ **d** $x^2 - 9x + 14$

2 Factorise these quadratic expressions.

    a $x^2 + 14x + 33$ **b** $x^2 + 4x - 32$ **c** $x^2 - 2x - 35$ **d** $x^2 - 5x - 36$

    e $x^2 + 3x - 70$ **f** $x^2 + 12x + 36$ **g** $x^2 - 16$ **h** $x^2 + 6x - 27$

TASK 6: Using identities

> ### ◉ Points to remember
>
> ◉ Two expressions are **identical** when their value is the same for any number,
>   e.g. $x^2 - y^2 \equiv (x + y)(x - y)$, where $\equiv$ means 'is identically equal to'.
> ◉ You can often prove that two expressions are identical using properties of geometrical shapes.

1. Use the identity $(x - y)(x + y) \equiv x^2 - y^2$ to work out the answers. Show your working.

   a $58^2 - 42^2$

   b $95^2 - 35^2$

   c $49^2 - 31^2$

   d $83^2 - 17^2$

   e $69^2 - 31^2$

   f $29^2 - 17^2$

2. Use the identity $(x + y)^2 \equiv x^2 + 2xy + y^2$ to work out the answers. Show your working.

   a 51^2 b 72^2 c 43^2 d 63^2 e 31^2 f 45^2

3. Use the identity $(x - y)^2 \equiv x^2 - 2xy + y^2$ to work out the answers. Show your working.

   a 69^2 b 28^2 c 57^2 d 76^2 e 38^2 f 49^2

TASK 7: Solving quadratic equations graphically

Points to remember

- A *quadratic equation* is of the form $y = ax^2 + bx + c$.
- The graph of a quadratic equation is a *U-shaped graph*.
- A quadratic graph may intersect the x-axis at two points, just touch the x-axis at one point or not touch the x-axis at all.
- Where a quadratic graph intersects or touches the x-axis, $y = 0$ and the values of x are the *solutions* or *roots* of $ax^2 + bx + c = 0$.

If you have a graph plotter or graphics calculator to use at home, do questions 1 and 2. If not, you need some graph paper. Do questions 1 and 3.

1. Write the equation of the graph you would draw to help you solve these equations.

   a $x^2 + 7x - 32 = 0$

   b $x^2 + 8x - 14 = 0$

2. Use a graph plotter or graphics calculator to draw the graphs to solve the equations below. Write the solutions to the equations in your book.

   a $x^2 - 3x - 10 = 0$

   b $x^2 - 2x - 24 = 0$

   c $x^2 + 3x - 28 = 0$

   d $x^2 - 6x - 16 = 0$

   e $x^2 - 3x - 18 = 0$

   f $x^2 + 2x - 35 = 0$

   Check your answers by substituting each value for x back into the original equation.

3 On graph paper, draw graphs to solve the equations below.
For each graph, complete this table of values.

x	-6	-4	-2	0	2	4	6
y							

Draw the x-axis from -5 to 5 and the y-axis from -10 to 10.

a $x^2 + 4x - 5 = 0$ 　　　　　　　　　b $x^2 - x - 6 = 0$

Check your solutions by substituting each value for x back into the original equation.

TASK 8: Sequences and patterns

● Points to remember

⊙ T_n is shorthand for the nth term of a sequence.

⊙ In a **linear sequence**, the difference between consecutive terms of a sequence is constant and T_n is a linear expression, e.g.

1, 4, 7, 10, 13, 16, … . Difference is 3, and $T_n = 3n - 2$

⊙ In a **quadratic sequence**, the first difference is not constant but the second difference is *constant*, and T_n is a quadratic expression, e.g.

1, 3, 6, 10, 15, 21, … . Second difference is 1, and $T_n = \dfrac{n(n+1)}{2}$

⊙ Substitute $n = 1, n = 2, n = 3, …$ into the nth term of a sequence to find the 1st, 2nd, 3rd, … terms.

1 Write the next three terms of these quadratic sequences.

a 7, 10, 15, 22, … 　　　　　　　　　b -1, 4, 11, 20, …

c 7, 11, 17, 25, … 　　　　　　　　　d 5, 14, 27, 44, …

2 Generate the first four terms of these quadratic sequences using their nth terms.

a $T_n = n^2 + 7$ 　　　　　　　　　b $T_n = n^2 + 5n$

c $T_n = n^2 + 3n - 2$ 　　　　　　　　　d $T_n = n^2 + 4n + 5$

3 Complete difference tables for these quadratic sequences and find their nth terms.

a 6, 14, 24, 36, … 　　　　　　　　　b $-7, -4, 1, 8, …$

c 2, 7, 14, 23, … 　　　　　　　　　d 8, 17, 28, 41, …

TASK 1: How long is that line?

> **Points to remember**
>
> ⊙ If you know the coordinates of the endpoints of a line segment, you can use Pythagoras' theorem to find its length.
>
> ⊙ The length of the line segment AB is $\sqrt{(x_B - x_A)^2 + (y_B - y_A)^2}$.
>
> B
> (x_B, y_B)
> A
> (x_A, y_A)

Where appropriate, give your answers to 1 decimal place.

1 Find the lengths of the line segments AB, CD, EF and GH.

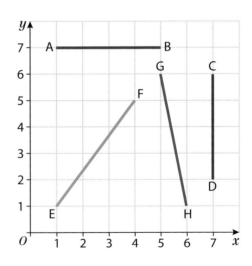

2 Find the length of the line segment FG joining the points F (3, 6) and G (5, 12).

3 Find the length of the line segment ST joining the points S (−7, 4) and G (−2, −8).

4 The points C (6, 3), D (9, 7) and E (13, 4) form a triangle.

    a Work out the lengths of CD, DE and CE.

    b What kind of triangle is triangle CDE?

TASK 2: Divide that line

Points to remember

⊙ To divide the line segment AB in a given ratio:

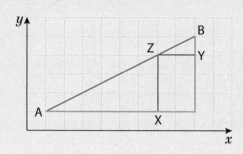

- draw a right-angled triangle with AB as hypotenuse;
- divide the base and height in the given ratio at points X and Y;
- draw lines through X and Y parallel to the axes to meet AB at Z;
- calculate the x- and y-coordinates of Z.

1 Write the coordinates of the midpoint of CD.

$\overline{\hspace{4cm}}$
C (3, 7)   D (9, 7)

2 Work out the coordinates of the point that divides IJ in the ratio 5 : 2.

$\overline{\hspace{4cm}}$
I (−3, 4)   J (11, 4)

3 Write the coordinates of the midpoint of LM.

4 Work out the coordinates of the point that divides PQ in the ratio 2 : 3.

M (−2, 15)

L (−2, 0)

P (9, 12)

Q (9, −13)

(5) Work out the coordinates of:

   a the midpoint of EF

   b the point that divides EF in the ratio 1:2

(6) Line QR has coordinates Q (−1, 3) and R (2, 15).

Work out the coordinates of:

   a the midpoint of QR

   b the point that divides QR in the ratio 2:4

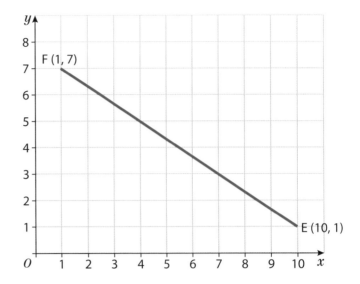

TASK 3: Enlargement

Points to remember

⊙ When a shape is enlarged, its angles stay the same. The object and image are **similar**.

⊙ **Scale factor** $= \dfrac{\text{length of side of image}}{\text{length of corresponding side of object}}$

⊙ Lines joining corresponding points of the object and image meet at the **centre of enlargement**.

⊙ When you enlarge a shape, measure distances of the vertices from the centre of enlargement. If C is the centre, for corresponding points P and P' on the object and image:

   CP' = scale factor × CP

⊙ For a scale factor between 0 and 1, the object is smaller than the image. It is still called an enlargement.

⊙ For a negative scale factor, the object and the image are on opposite sides of the centre of enlargement.

⊙ When a perimeter is enlarged it is multiplied by the scale factor.

You will need some squared paper.

(1) An object has a perimeter of 30 m. It is enlarged by a scale factor of 0.7. What is the perimeter of the enlarged image?

2 Write:

   a the coordinates of the centre of enlargement

   b the scale factor for this enlargement

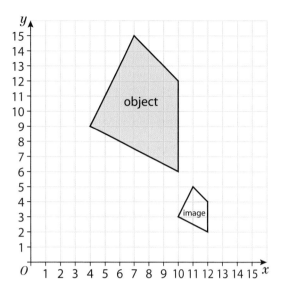

3 Copy each diagram on squared paper.
The centre of enlargement is marked with a dot.

   a On the same copy of the diagram, draw enlargements with:

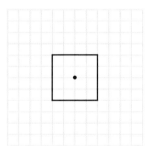

     i scale factor 2
    ii scale factor 0.5

   b On the same copy of the diagram, draw enlargements with:

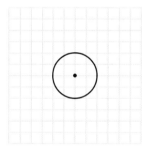

     i scale factor 3
    ii scale factor $\frac{1}{2}$

4 Copy the diagram on squared paper.

Enlarge triangle P with a scale factor of -3, centre (5, 6).

Label the image Q.

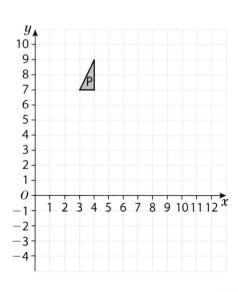

TASK 4: Rotation

 Points to remember

- When a shape is rotated, its lengths and angles stay the same. The object and image are **congruent**.
- Use tracing paper to rotate shapes and to find the centre of rotation.
- A rotation is described by giving:
  - the **centre of rotation**;
  - the **angle of rotation** in degrees or as a fraction of a turn;
  - the **direction** of the rotation, clockwise or anticlockwise.

Example

Rotate the pink triangle a quarter turn clockwise about the point A.

- Use tracing paper.
- Trace the shape of the object. Mark point A.
- Fix point A with a pencil or compass point so that it does not move.
- Turn the tracing paper about A, clockwise through 90°.
- The new position of the shape is the image.

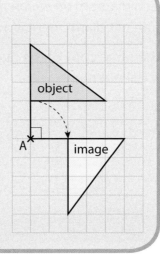

You will need squared paper, tracing paper, ruler and pencil.

1. **a** Describe fully the rotation that maps shape A onto:

   i shape B   **ii** shape C   **iii** shape D

   b Describe fully the rotation that maps shape B onto shape A.

   c Describe fully the rotation that maps shape B onto shape D.

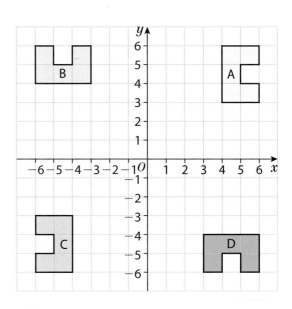

The Life Of William Shakespeare QUIZ

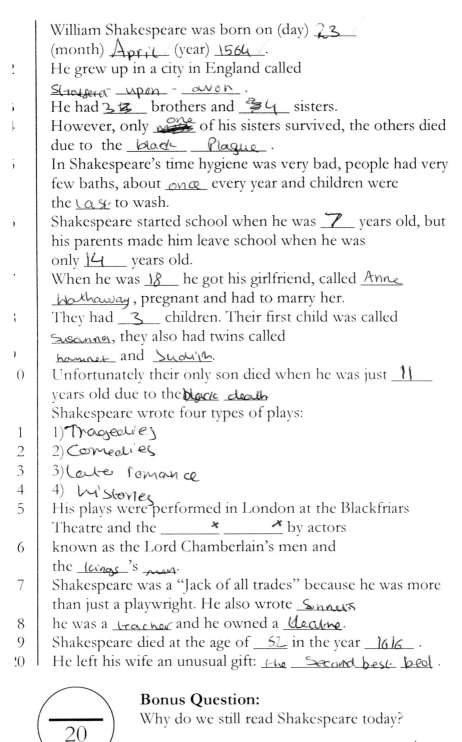

William Shakespeare was born on (day) 23
(month) April (year) 1564.
He grew up in a city in England called
Stratford - upon - avon .
He had 3 brothers and 4 sisters.
However, only one of his sisters survived, the others died
due to the black Plague .
In Shakespeare's time hygiene was very bad, people had very
few baths, about once every year and children were
the lay to wash.
Shakespeare started school when he was 7 years old, but
his parents made him leave school when he was
only 14 years old.
When he was 18 he got his girlfriend, called Anne
Hathaway, pregnant and had to marry her.
They had 3 children. Their first child was called
Susanna, they also had twins called
hamnet and Judith.
Unfortunately their only son died when he was just 11
years old due to the black death
Shakespeare wrote four types of plays:
1) Tragedies
2) Comedies
3) Late romance
4) Histories
His plays were performed in London at the Blackfriars
Theatre and the ____ ✗ ____ ✗ by actors
known as the Lord Chamberlain's men and
the kings 's men.
Shakespeare was a "Jack of all trades" because he was more
than just a playwright. He also wrote Sonnets
he was a teacher and he owned a theatre.
Shakespeare died at the age of 52 in the year 1616 .
He left his wife an unusual gift: the second best bed .

(20)

Bonus Question:
Why do we still read Shakespeare today?
_____ .

② Copy the diagram on squared paper.

a Rotate shape A 180° about the origin O. Label the image B.

b Rotate shape A 90° clockwise about O. Label the image C.

c Rotate shape A 90° anticlockwise about O. Label the image D.

You may use tracing paper to help you.

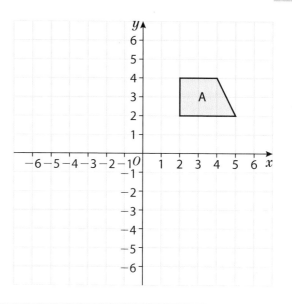

TASK 5: Combining transformations

 Points to remember

⊙ For **rotation**, **translation** and **reflection**, the image is congruent to the object; for **enlargement**, the image is similar to the object.

⊙ Repeated rotations about the same centre of rotation can be replaced by a single rotation.

⊙ Repeated translations can be replaced by a single translation.

⊙ Rotation, translation, reflection and enlargement can be combined in any order to transform an object.

⊙ It is sometimes possible to find a single transformation which has the same effect as a combination of transformations.

⊙ Different combinations of transformations can have the same effect.

⊙ In any combination of transformations, the angles and symmetries of the object are unchanged.

You will need squared paper, tracing paper, ruler and pencil.

① Copy this diagram on squared paper.

a Reflect the quadrilateral in the line $x = 3$, then reflect the image in the line $x = 6$.

b Describe fully the single transformation which maps the quadrilateral onto the final image.

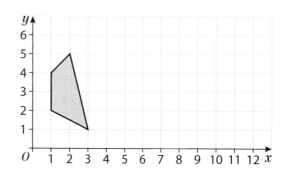

② Draw the x-axis from 0 to 6 and the y-axis from -10 to 5.
Draw the same quadrilateral in the same position as in question 1.

    a Reflect the quadrilateral in the line $x = 3$, then reflect the image in the line $y = -2$.

    b Describe fully the single transformation which maps the quadrilateral onto the final image.

③ Draw the x-axis from 0 to 10 and the y-axis from 0 to 10.
Draw the same quadrilateral in the same position as in question 1.

    a Translate the quadrilateral 4 units up, then rotate the image 90° clockwise about (5, 5).

    b Describe fully the single transformation which maps the quadrilateral onto the final image.

④ Draw the x-axis from 0 to 12 and the y-axis from 0 to 12.
Draw the same quadrilateral in the same position as in question 1.

    a Rotate the shape 90° anticlockwise about centre (4, 7), then rotate the image 90° clockwise about centre (10, 6).

    b Describe fully the single transformation which maps the quadrilateral onto the final image.

TASK 6: Loci 1

⦿ Points to remember

⊙ A **locus** is the set of points that satisfy given conditions.

⊙ In 2D, the locus of all points that are:
- a given distance from a fixed point is a circle;
- equidistant from a line segment is a shape formed by two parallel lines joined at each end by a semicircle;

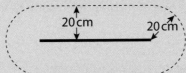

- equidistant from the arms of an angle is the bisector of the angle;
- equidistant from two points is the perpendicular bisector of the line segment joining the two points.

⊙ Construction lines and arcs should be visible and not be rubbed out.

You will need a pair of compasses, protractor, ruler and pencil.

① Draw a line segment 4 cm long.
Draw the locus of all the points that are 3 cm away from the line.

(2) Draw two points A and B that are 4 cm apart.
Draw the locus of all the points that are equidistant from A and B.

(3) Draw the locus of all the points that are 4 cm from a point C.

(4) The pendulum on a clock swings from side to side.
The pendulum is 30 cm long and swings 20° on either side of the vertical.

Draw the locus of the end of the pendulum.
Use a scale of 1 to 5.

TASK 7: Loci 2

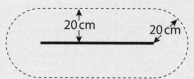

⊙ Points to remember

- ⊙ The locus of points equidistant from a line segment is a shape formed by two parallel lines joined at each end by a semicircle.

- ⊙ A locus can define a region, e.g. the set of points that are less than 20 cm from a line segment is the region inside the dashed line below.

20 cm   20 cm

- ⊙ More than one locus can define a region that complies with all the conditions.

You will need squared paper, a pair of compasses, ruler and pencil.

(1) Vivian ties a sheep to the wall of a barn in the middle of a field.
She uses a length of rope 7 m long.
The sheep is tethered 2 m from the corner of the barn.

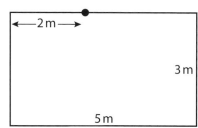

←—2 m—→

3 m

5 m

a On squared paper, make a scale drawing of the barn.
Choose a suitable scale to use.

b Draw and shade the area of grass that the sheep can eat.

2 Three television masts each transmit signals over a radius of 100 km.

Copy the diagram below on centimetre squared paper.

Using a scale of 1 cm to represent 20 km, draw and shade the area showing the points that do not receive a signal from one of the three masts.

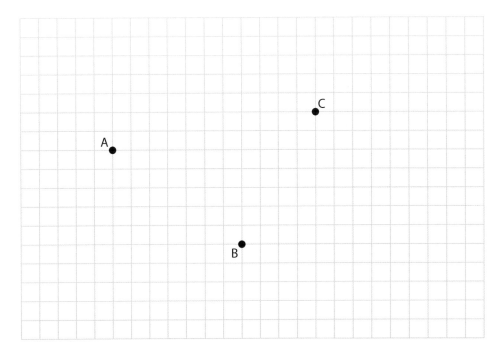

Decimals and accuracy

TASK 1: Recurring decimals

⦿ Points to remember

- ⦿ Fractions whose denominators have only 2s or 5s as their prime factors convert to **terminating decimals**.
- ⦿ Other fractions convert to **recurring decimals**.
- ⦿ Convert terminating decimals to fractions by expressing them as tenths, hundredths or thousandths.
- ⦿ Use algebra to convert recurring decimals to fractions.
- ⦿ Some decimals cannot be converted to an exact fraction, e.g. π. These are called **irrational numbers**.

1. Write each fraction as a recurring decimal. You may use your calculator.

   a $\frac{19}{33}$ b $\frac{85}{101}$ c $\frac{2}{9}$ d $\frac{3}{7}$

2. Write each terminating decimal as a fraction in its simplest form.

   a 0.75   b 0.375   c 0.175   d 0.245

3. Write each recurring decimal as a fraction in its simplest form.

   a $0.\dot{1}\dot{5}$ b $0.\dot{8}$ c $0.2\dot{7}\dot{6}$ d $0.\dot{5}\dot{4}$

TASK 2: Significant figures

⦿ Points to remember

- ⦿ The first **significant figure** of a number is its first non-zero digit.
- ⦿ A number rounded to one significant figure has only one non-zero digit.
- ⦿ In general, estimates of calculations are made by rounding numbers to one significant figure. Sometimes other approximations of the numbers in a calculation are more sensible.

1. Estimate the answers by rounding each number to one significant figure.

   a 0.83×493

   b $918 \div 0.29$

   c $846 \div 0.39$

   d 0.77×0.048

   e $(42 \times 2.6) \div 0.478$

   f $(2.8 + 6.1) \times (0.54 - 0.19)$

2. Work out an estimate for the value of $\dfrac{34.8 \times 88.8}{0.49}$.

3. Write these numbers correct to 2 significant figures.

   a 456

   b $0.006\,77$

TASK 3: Using a calculator

Points to remember

- Make sure you can use your calculator efficiently, including the function keys for fractions, brackets, π, square root, square, powers, negative numbers and the memory.
- A string of multiplications and divisions can be entered into a calculator in one go; there is no need to work out each step separately.
- When you do an **exact calculation**, round the final answer, not the intermediate steps.
- Don't give too many figures in answers. In general, the answer should not have more significant figures (s.f.) than those in the problem. 2 or 3 s.f. are usually enough.

1. Use a calculator to work out these.
   Give each answer to a suitable degree of accuracy.

   a $2.42^2 + (6.7 - 1.04)^2$

   b $\dfrac{43.5 \times 21.3}{4.6 \times (8.3 - 2.68)}$

   c $4\frac{5}{8} - 2\frac{11}{12}$

   d $2.7^5 \times 0.9^4$

   e $\sqrt[3]{4.8 \times 2.5}$

   f $\dfrac{3.5 \times 10^4}{0.7 \times 10^{-2}}$

2. What is the smallest whole number that you can add to a million to make the answer exactly divisible by 9731?

TASK 4: Back of an envelope calculations

Points to remember

- **Approximate calculations** can provide good estimates.
- Approximate calculations are often called 'back of an envelope' calculations because they are easy enough to work out on the back of an envelope.
- When you do approximate calculations, you can round the numbers at any stage of the calculation.
- To estimate measurements, it helps to know some 'benchmarks', e.g. the approximate height of a door (2 m) or the capacity of a tea cup (200 ml).

(1) Which competition prize will use about 1 000 000 seconds of your time?

    A One week at Disney World

    B 10 days in Spain

    C A fortnight skiing

    D A month on a cruise

    E A year on a trip around the world

    Explain your answer.

(2) Could you write your name and address on a piece of paper with an area of 0.01 square metres? Explain your answer.

(3) A fast sprinter runs a 100 metre race in about 10 seconds.

Could you drive safely through a large town at the speed of a sprinter?

Explain your answer.

TASK 5: Measurement errors

Points to remember

- Measurements may be inaccurate by up to half a unit in either direction, e.g. '4 kg to the nearest kilogram' has a least possible weight of 3.5 kg and a greatest possible weight of 4.5 kg.
- The **lower bound** is the least possible value of the measurement and the **upper bound** is the greatest possible value of the measurement.
- For **continuous quantities**, such as heights, the value of the measurement can equal the lower bound but not the upper bound.
- For **discrete quantities**, such as numbers of objects, the value of the number can equal the lower bound or the upper bound.

1. Copy and complete this table to show the lower and upper bounds of the measurements.
   Each measurement is to the nearest whole unit.

Measurement	Lower bound	Upper bound
15 litres		
124 cm		
8.5 m		
83.2 cm		
0.8 kg		
10 seconds		

2. Peter weighs himself and his dog.
   He weighs 52 kg. His dog weighs 14 kg.
   Both measurements are to the nearest kg.

   Explain why their minimum combined weight could be 65 kg.

3. A square has sides of length 8.5 cm correct to the nearest millimetre.

   Calculate:

   a the lower bound of the perimeter

   b the upper bound of the area

Probability 1

TASK 1: Relative frequency

Points to remember

- If an event occurs N times in T trials, its **relative frequency** is $\frac{N}{T}$, or

$$\text{relative frequency} = \frac{\text{number of times the event occurs}}{\text{total number of trials}}$$

- Relative frequency can be written as a fraction, a decimal or a percentage.
- The probability of an event can be estimated by doing an experiment.
- Experimental probability can be equated to relative frequency.
- If the probability of an event is p, and there are to be T trials of an experiment, the event is likely to occur an estimated $p \times T$ times.

1. Ali records the colour of cars as they pass the school gate on three different days. The results are shown in this table.

	Number of cars that are						Total number of cars observed
	Red	Black	Blue	Silver	White	Other	
Mon	3	1	9	20	7	10	50
Tue	12	5	33	53	25	22	150
Wed	18	8	44	102	31	47	250

Copy and complete this table of relative frequencies of the different coloured cars.

	Relative frequency of cars that are					
	Red	Black	Blue	Silver	White	Other
Mon	0.06					
Tue						
Wed						

② Some pupils do an experiment with a dice to see if it is a fair dice.
The dice has four red faces and two blue faces.

Each pupil rolls the dice a different number of times and records its colour.
The results are shown in this table.

Name	Number of rolls	Number of red faces rolled	Number of blue faces rolled
Ricky	20	16	4
Saeed	60	38	22
Lucy	100	64	36
Mary	180	118	62

a Work out the relative frequency of rolling a red for each pupil's results.

b Work out the theoretical probability of rolling a red.

c In which pupil's experiment would you expect the relative frequency to give the best estimate of the probability of rolling a red face? Explain your answer.

d Use all the pupils' results to estimate the probability of rolling a blue.
Compare this with the theoretical probability of rolling a blue.

TASK 2: Exploring relative frequency

 Points to remember

⊙ With repeated trials or observations, relative frequency tends to a limit, which can be shown in a **relative frequency graph**.

⊙ For equally likely outcomes, the values of relative frequencies (experimental probabilities) approach theoretical probabilities as the number of trials becomes large.

⊙ When outcomes are not equally likely, relative frequency is used to estimate probability.

You need a copy of **S6.2 Resource sheet 2.2**.

Complete the two questions on the sheet.

TASK 3: Combined events

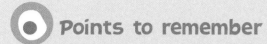

Points to remember

⊙ Two or more events can occur at the same time or one after the other.
⊙ The outcomes of a trial involving two combined events can be shown by using **systematic listing**, a **two-way table** or a **tree diagram**.

1　**a**　Copy and complete this two-way table to show all the possible outcomes when two cards are picked from a standard pack of playing cards.

First card

Second card		♥(H)	♣(C)	♦(D)	♠(S)
	♥(H)	HH	CH		
	♣(C)				
	♦(D)				
	♠(S)				

　b　Represent the same information on a tree diagram.

2　To decide who starts a game, Leroy and Ella each roll a dice.
If one of the numbers rolled is odd and the other is even, Leroy starts the game. Otherwise, Ella starts the game.

　a　Explain why Leroy rolling the dice and Ella rolling the dice are independent events.

　b　Copy and complete this list of all the possible outcomes when Leroy and Ella roll the dice.

　　Odd and odd
　　Odd and ………
　　…………………

　c　Show all the possible outcomes in a two-way table.

　d　Draw a tree diagram to show all the possible outcomes.

　e　**i**　Explain why each possible outcome is equally likely.

　　　ii　Explain why this is a fair way to decide who starts the game.

TASK 4: Tree diagrams and independent events

1. Tim has a pack containing equal numbers of these two cards.

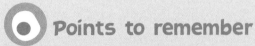

Fay has a pack containing equal numbers of these three cards.

a. Tim picks one of his cards at random. Fay picks one of her cards at random.

Copy and complete this tree diagram to show all the possible outcomes of the trial.

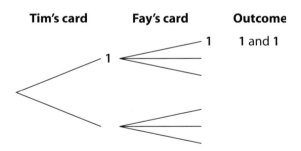

b. Write the probabilities of each outcome on the branches of the diagram.

c. Explain why the probability of each of the combined outcomes is $\frac{1}{6}$.

d. The card picked at random from Tim's pack does not affect the card picked at random from Fay's pack. What sort of events are these?

e. Kevin and Naomi add the numbers on the cards to obtain a score.

   i. Explain why the probability of a score of 3 is equal to the probability of a score of 4.

   ii. What is the probability of a score of 3 or 4?

2. For each of these pairs of events decide whether or not it is likely that the events are independent. Give a reason for each of your answers.

a Event **A** There are gales on Friday morning.
Event **B** There are gales on Friday afternoon.

b Event **C** There are gales on a Friday in April.
Event **D** There are gales on a Friday in November.

c Two coins are thrown.
Event **E** One coin shows heads.
Event **F** The other coin shows heads.

d Sally's mum gives her a lift to school.
Event **G** The car breaks down.
Event **H** Sally is late for school.

TASK 5: Probability experiments

Points to remember

⊙ If A and B are independent events, the probability of A and B occurring is P(A) × P(B).

⊙ The connection between probability and relative frequency after a large number of trials holds for trials involving two independent events.

1. Jack travels on the same bus each morning, including weekends. Each day the probability that the bus will be on time is $\frac{5}{6}$. Estimate the number of days that the bus will be on time in June.

2. A dice is thrown 600 times.

a If it is a fair dice, how many times would you expect it to land on the number 4?

b If the dice is biased and it lands on either 1, 2, 3, 4 or 5 on 400 of the throws:

i What is the relative frequency of the dice landing on 6?

ii Estimate the probability that it will land on 6.

3 A bag contains 8 counters: 5 red counters and 3 blue counters.
A box contains 10 bricks; 6 of the bricks are blue, the rest are red.

A counter is picked at random from the bag and a brick is picked at random from the box.

a Draw a probability tree diagram.

Use the tree diagram from part **a** to answer these questions.

b What is the probability that the counter will be red and the brick will be blue?

c What is the probability that the counter and the brick are the same colour?

d What is the probability that the counter and the brick are different colours?

e What is the probability that at least one item will be red?

4 A fair spinner has coloured sectors that are equal in area. Some of the sectors are the same colour.

The spinner is spun 100 times.
The number of times it lands on red is recorded after every 20 spins.
The results are shown in the table.

Number of spins	20	40	60	80	100
Frequency of red	6	10	15	22	26
Relative frequency	0.3				

a Copy and complete the table.

b What is the best estimate of the probability of landing on red?

c How many times would you expect the spinner to land on red in 2000 spins?

d Two sectors of the spinner are coloured red.
How many sectors do you think there are altogether?
Explain your answer.

Measures and mensuration

TASK 1: Arcs of circles

Points to remember

⊙ **Circumference** of a circle = $\pi \times$ diameter = $2 \times \pi \times$ radius

⊙ **Length of arc** = (angle of arc ÷ 360°) × circumference of circle
= (angle of arc ÷ 360°) × $\pi \times$ diameter
= (angle of arc ÷ 360°) × $2 \times \pi \times$ radius

Give all your answers to 1 decimal place.

1. Calculate the arc length of each of these sectors.

a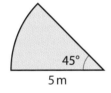
45°
5 m

b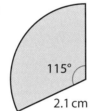
115°
2.1 cm

c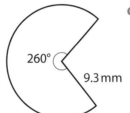
260°
9.3 mm

d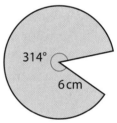
314°
6 cm

2. A discus landing area is in the form of a sector of a circle with a radius of 80 m and an angle at the centre of 40°.

   Calculate the perimeter of the landing area.

3. Calculate the perimeter of this shape.

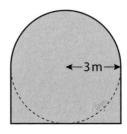
←3 m→

TASK 2: Sectors of circles

Write all your answers to 1 decimal place.

1 Work out the areas of these sectors.

a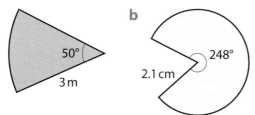
50°
3 m

b
248°
2.1 cm

c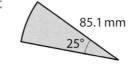
85.1 mm
25°

d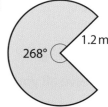
1.2 m
268°

2 A javelin landing area is in the shape of a sector of a circle with radius 95 m and an angle at the centre of 29°.

29°
95 m

What is the total area of the landing area?

3 At a summer fete, competitors must throw a beanbag so that it lands in the shaded part of the sector.

Work out the shaded area.

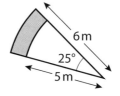
6 m
25°
5 m

TASK 3: Prisms and cylinders

Points to remember

- A **prism** is a solid with two parallel *bases* that are congruent polygons. Cross-sections parallel to a base are identical to the base.
- A **cylinder** is a solid with two parallel bases that are identical circles. Cross-sections parallel to a base are circles identical to the base.
- Volume of a prism = area of cross-section × length
- Volume of a cylinder = area of cross-section × length
  = π × radius × radius × length
- The **surface area of a solid** is the sum of the areas of all the faces.

1. This table shows the volumes of some cuboids. Write the missing measurements.

	Length	Width	Height	Volume
a	?	2 m	1.5 m	30 m³
b	12 mm	?	1.2 mm	144 mm³
c	24 cm	0.5 cm	?	6 cm³

2. Calculate the volume of this triangular prism.

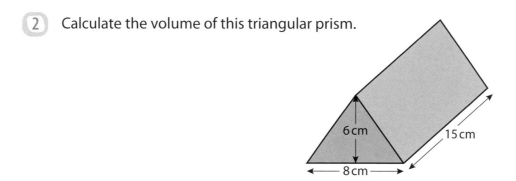

3. The cross-section of a pentagonal prism has an area of 34 mm².
   The prism is 25 mm long.
   Calculate the volume of the prism.

4. A cylinder has a radius of 4 mm and a length of 25 mm.
   Calculate the volume of the cylinder.
   Give your answer to 1 decimal place.

5. A cuboid is 6 m long and has a volume of 180 m³.
   What is the area of its cross-section?

TASK 4: Units of area and volume

Points to remember

- In area or volume problems, make sure that the sides or edges of shapes are in the same unit.
- $1\,cm^2 = (10\,mm)^2 = 100\,mm^2 = 1 \times 10^2\,mm^2$
- $1\,m^2 = (100\,cm)^2 = 10\,000\,cm^2 = 1 \times 10^4\,cm^2$
- $1\,m^2 = (1000\,mm)^2 = 1\,000\,000\,mm^2 = 1 \times 10^6\,mm^2$
- $1\,cm^3 = (10\,mm)^3 = 1000\,mm^3 = 1 \times 10^3\,mm^3$
- $1\,m^3 = (100\,cm)^3 = 1\,000\,000\,cm^3 = 1 \times 10^6\,cm^3$
- $1\,m^3 = (1000\,mm)^3 = 1\,000\,000\,000\,mm^3 = 1 \times 10^9\,mm^3$
- **1 litre** = 1000 ml = 1000 cm³

1.   **a** Change 3 m² into cm².   **b** Change 1.7 cm² into mm².

     c Change 4 m² into mm².   **d** Change 5 cm² into m².

     e Change 6 km² into m².

2.   **a** Change 5 m³ into cm³.   **b** Change 6 cm³ into mm³.

     c Change 4.3 cm³ into mm³.   **d** Change 0.09 m³ into cm³.

     e Change 2 km³ into m³.

3. Lake Superior in North America has the largest surface area of any freshwater lake in the world.

     a The surface area of the lake is approximately 8.2×10^{10} m².

       How many km² is this?

     b Lake Superior holds approximately 12 100 km³ of water.

       How many cubic metres is this?

Lake Superior

TASK 5: Plans and elevations

Points to remember

⊙ The **plan** is a view of the object from directly above.

⊙ An **elevation** is a view of the object from the side or the front.

⊙ A sphere and a cube each have the same plan view, front elevation and side elevation.

You will need squared paper.

① This shape is made from 7 cubes.

The front elevation is coloured green.

On squared paper, draw a plan and side and front elevations for the shape.

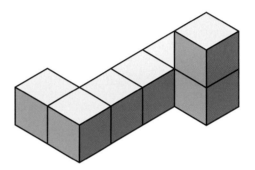

② This shape is made from 7 cubes.
The front and the side views are labelled.

On squared paper, draw a plan and side and front elevations for the shape.

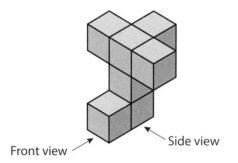

Front view   Side view

③ The diagrams below show the plan views of five solids.
Describe what each solid could be. Give your reasons.

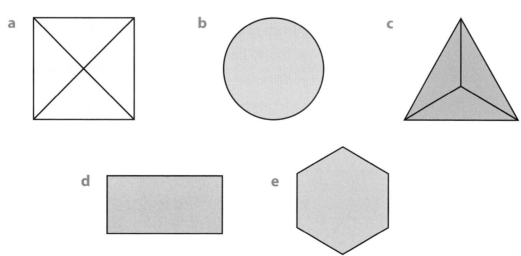

a   b   c

d   e

TASK 1: Biased data

> ### ⊙ Points to remember
>
> - A **population** is the whole set of individuals or items studied in a statistical investigation.
> - A **sample** is a selection from a population used to find out about the population without studying all of it.
> - A **representative sample** is not biased towards any group in the population.
> - A **biased sample** favours one section of the population more than another.
> - In a **random sample** each item has an equal chance of being chosen. It may not be representative.

1. There are 420 houses in a village.

   There are 73 detached houses, 123 bungalows, 84 semi-detached houses and 140 terraced houses.

   Francesca lives in a street of semi-detached houses.

   She plans to ask the residents of a sample of 40 houses what they can do to support the village in a Tidy Village competition.

   a Describe the population for this survey.

   b Comment on each of these methods of sampling the population.

   Method A Francesca chooses the 40 houses closest to her own house.

   Method B Francesca chooses 40 houses at random.

   Method C Francesca chooses 10 of each sort of house at random.

   c Explain why in a representative sample of the houses in the village there should be more terraced houses than semi-detached houses.

2 Tina is investigating the amount of time that pupils in her school spend doing homework.

    a What is the population in this investigation?

    b Tina asks pupils in her maths set during Thursday's lesson this question:

> How long did you spend doing homework last night?

    Give three reasons why this method is likely to produce biased data.

    c Describe two ways in which Tina could improve her sample.

3 A magazine publishes a questionnaire about attitudes to fox hunting.
They ask their readers to complete the questionnaire and send it to them.

    a Explain why the results are likely to be biased.

    b Describe a better method of asking people to complete the questionnaire.

TASK 2: Minimising bias

 Points to remember

To **minimise bias** in a statistical investigation:

⊙ avoid questions that suggest that a particular answer is correct;

⊙ choose a representative sample by including groups in the same proportions as in the population as a whole;

⊙ choose the items for each group in the representative sample at random.

1 Give a reason why each of the following questions is biased.

> Big Brother is a fantastic TV programme, isn't it?

> The Queen should pay tax, shouldn't she?

> Classical music is rubbish. Don't you agree?

Rewrite each question in a way that minimises bias.

2 Meg wants to find out what people in Finkley think about the sports facilities in the town.
She is going to stand outside the Finkley sports centre one Friday morning.
She plans to ask people going into the sports centre to complete a questionnaire.

    a Give one reason why Meg's survey will be biased.

    b Describe one change Meg could make to the way in which she is going to carry out her survey so that it will be less biased.

(3) Samman is carrying out a survey of pupils in his school.
He wants to find out what they think about motorbikes.

He plans to ask a representative sample of 10% of the school to complete a questionnaire.

The size of each year group in his school is shown in this table.

Year	7	8	9	10	11	Total
Boys	81	92	79	74	82	**398**
Girls	79	68	81	86	78	**402**
Total	160	160	160	160	160	**800**

a Explain why the numbers in Samman's sample in each year group should be the same.

b Explain why the total number of boys and total number of girls in the sample should be the same.

c Explain why the number of boys and number of girls sampled from Year 8 should **not** be the same.

d In which other year group should the number of boys and number of girls sampled **not** be the same?

e Calculate the number of boys and girls in each year group in the sample.

f Describe how the actual pupils in the sample in each year group might be chosen.

TASK 3: Frequency polygons

 Points to remember

⊙ Large sets of data are organised in groups to make the data more manageable.

⊙ Grouped data can be represented in a grouped frequency table and a frequency polygon.

⊙ To draw a frequency polygon:
  – plot the midpoints of class intervals against frequency;
  – join the points with straight lines.

⊙ The midpoint of the range $0 \leqslant x < 20$ is 10 for continuous data and 9.5 for discrete data.

You will need graph paper.

① This grouped frequency table represents the times, t, that 50 pupils take to complete ten pull-ups.

Draw a frequency polygon to represent this data.

Time (t, seconds)	Frequency
$0 \leqslant t < 20$	3
$20 \leqslant t < 40$	13
$40 \leqslant t < 60$	27
$60 \leqslant t < 80$	6
$80 \leqslant t < 100$	1

② The grouped frequency table shows the distribution of ages of the first 100 cars entering a multistorey car park.

Age in years	0 to 1	2 to 3	4 to 5	6 to 7	8 to 9	10 to 11
Frequency	19	32	23	13	9	4

Draw a frequency polygon to represent the ages of these cars.

③ This frequency polygon shows the time taken for a representative sample of children to travel to school.

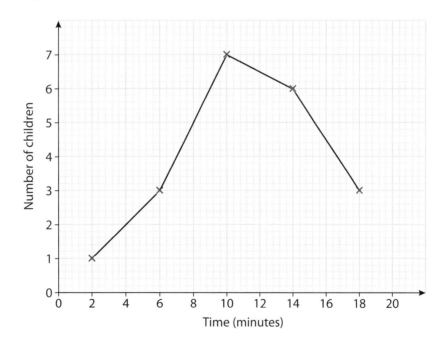

a How many children are in the sample?

b How many children take less than 12 minutes to travel to school?
Explain your answer.

c How many children take more than 16 minutes to travel to school?
Explain your answer.

TASK 4: Estimating the mean of grouped data

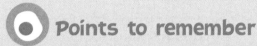
Points to remember

⊙ Accurate values of average and spread cannot be calculated for grouped data but estimates can be made.

⊙ An **estimate of the mean** can be calculated from:

$$\Sigma(f \times x) \div \Sigma f$$

where: Σ is a symbol meaning 'the sum of'

x represents the midpoint of each class interval

f represents the frequency

1 Calculate an estimate of the mean for the sets of data in Task 3, questions 1, 2 and 3.

TASK 5: Average and range of grouped data

Points to remember

⊙ The **median** value in a set of n ordered values is:
 – the $\frac{1}{2}(n + 1)$th value when n is odd;
 – the mean of the $\frac{1}{2}n$th and $(\frac{1}{2}n + 1)$th values when n is even.

⊙ For grouped data, you can work out which interval contains the median by using the running total of the frequencies.

⊙ To estimate the median, assume that the data is evenly spread throughout the class interval in which the median occurs.

⊙ The **modal class** of a set of grouped data is the class interval with the greatest frequency.

⊙ The **spread** of a set of grouped data can be estimated by making an estimate of the **range**.

⊙ Measures of average (mean, median, mode) and spread (range) can be estimated from a frequency polygon.

1 For each set of data in Task 3, questions 1, 2 and 3:

  a Find the modal class.

  b i Find the class interval containing the median.

    ii Calculate an estimate of the median.

  c Calculate an estimate of the range.

TASK 6: Correlation

Points to remember

⊙ A **scatter graph** is used to show whether there is a relationship between two variables.

⊙ A **line of best fit** is a straight line that represents the best estimate of the relationship between the two variables on a scatter graph.

⊙ When you draw a line of best fit, there should be roughly equal numbers of points on the scatter graph on each side of the line.

⊙ **Correlation** is a measure of the strength of the relationship between two variables. High correlation occurs when there is a close relationship and the points of the scatter graph lie close to the line of best fit.

⊙ The correlation is positive when an increase in one variable results in an increase in the other, negative when an increase in one variable results in a decrease in the other, and zero when there is no clear relationship between the variables and a line of best fit cannot be drawn.

You will need graph paper.

1   **a**   Which of the scatter graphs below show:

     i positive correlation   **ii** no correlation   **iii** negative correlation?

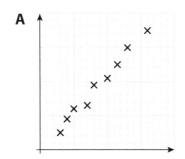

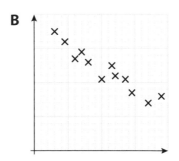

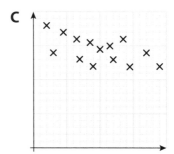

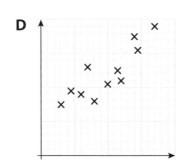

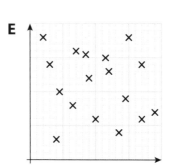

   b   In which of the scatter graphs is the correlation the strongest?

(2) Tom tests how high he can jump on BMX bikes of different weights.

The table below shows his results.

Weight (kg)	Height (cm)
8.0	26.8
8.5	26.4
9.0	26.1
9.5	25.7
10.0	25.0
10.5	24.8
11.0	24.3

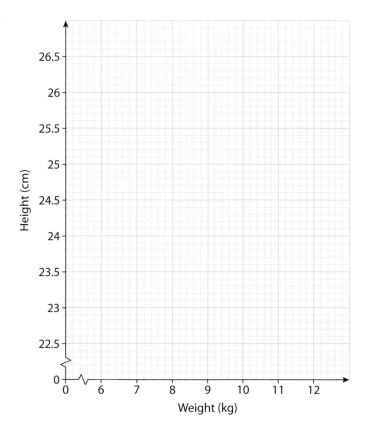

a Copy the grid on the right on graph paper. Draw a scatter graph to show the results.

b Draw a line of best fit.

c i Estimate the height Tom can jump on a bike weighing 9.7 kg.

ii Tom jumps 24.5 cm.
Estimate the weight of the bike he is using.

d Describe what happens to the height Tom can jump as the weight he carries increases.

e Describe the correlation between the weight of the bike and the height of the jump. Choose from:

A High positive correlation   B High negative correlation

C Low positive correlation   D Low negative correlation   E No correlation

TASK 7a: Statistical investigation

Points to remember

⊙ To carry out a **statistical investigation,** follow the steps in the **data handling cycle**.

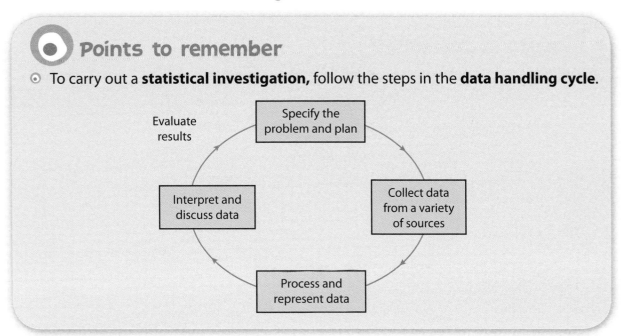

Do either question 1 or question 2.

1. Continue your comparison of one of these:

   a people's hand spans with their shoe sizes;

   b reaction times of two different groups of pupils;

   c people's ability to estimate lengths of lines (straight and curved) and sizes of angles;

   d word lengths and sentence lengths in two different newspapers;

   e percentage scores in tests in different subjects;

   f your own investigation.

   Think about what you need to do to process and represent your data.
   You could start to draw some graphs, or calculate estimates of average and spread.

2. Emma wants to investigate the amount of money pupils in her school spend and save.
   She decides to investigate these hypotheses.

   Hypothesis 1

   > On average, pupils in year 11 spend more each week than pupils in year 9.

   Hypothesis 2

   > Pupils who have more income from pocket money and/or part time jobs save more.

   Write a detailed list of what Emma needs to do to carry out her investigation in order to:

   a collect data from a variety of sources;

   b process and represent data.

TASK 7b: Statistical investigation

Points to remember

⊙ To complete a **statistical investigation**, follow the steps in the data handling cycle.

Evaluate results

Specify the problem and plan

Interpret and discuss data

Collect data from a variety of sources

Process and represent data

1. Emma is investigating the amount of money pupils in her school spend and save.

   She bases her investigation on these hypotheses.

   ### Hypothesis 1

   On average, pupils in Year 11 spend more each week than pupils in Year 9.

   ### Hypothesis 2

   Pupils who have more income from pocket money and/or part time jobs save more.

   Emma collects a representative sample of data from Year 9 and Year 11.

   a Emma draws these two frequency polygons.

Frequency polygon to show average weekly expenditure of pupils in Year 11

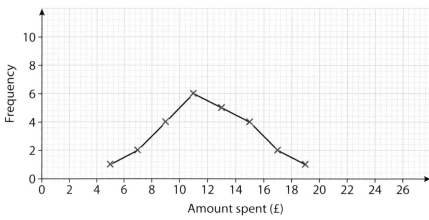

Frequency polygon to show average weekly expenditure of pupils in Year 9

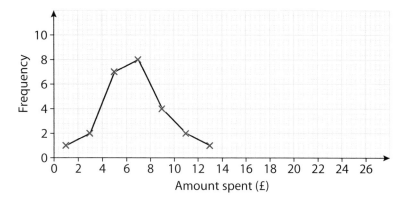

i Use the two frequency polygons to calculate measures of average and spread for Years 9 and Year 11.

ii What comments should Emma make about the measures of average and spread and the frequency polygons?

iii What conclusion should she make about Hypothesis 1?

b Emma also draws these two scatter graphs.

Scatter graph showing income and savings for pupils in Year 9

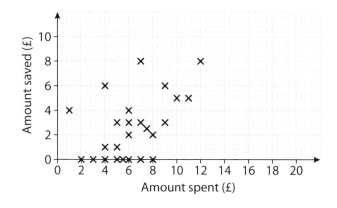

Scatter graph showing income and savings for pupils in Year 11

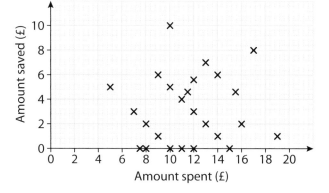

i Comment on the correlation shown in the two scatter graphs.

ii What conclusion should Emma make about Hypothesis 2?

Trigonometry 2

TASK 1: Using Pythagoras' theorem 1

⊙ Points to remember

- **Pythagorean triples** are sets of three integers that satisfy the relationship $a^2 + b^2 = c^2$: for example, 3, 4, 5 or 5, 12, 13.
- **Pythagoras' theorem** can be written as a formula, $a^2 + b^2 = c^2$, where a and b are the lengths of the two shorter sides of a right-angled triangle and c is the length of the hypotenuse.
- If you know the lengths of the two shorter sides of a right-angled triangle, use Pythagoras' theorem to find the length of the hypotenuse.

Example

Find length a.

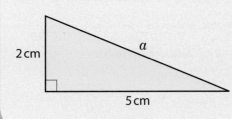

Using Pythagoras' theorem:

$2^2 + 5^2 = a^2$

$4 + 25 = a^2$

$29 = a^2$

$\sqrt{29} = a$

$a = 5.39$ cm (correct to 3 s.f.)

Use your calculator.

① This is a list of some random numbers:

19 22 42 31 30 33 15 34 32 13 37 47 43 49 14 18 9 38 3 40

a   Pick any three numbers from the list.
Use them as the side lengths of a triangle.
Use Pythagoras' theorem to see if the triangle is right-angled.
Repeat this twice more.

b   9 and 40 are in the list.
What other integer needs to be in the list to make a Pythagorean triple?

c   30 and 40 are in the list.
What other integer needs to be in the list to make a Pythagorean triple?

TASK 2: Using Pythagoras' theorem 2

 Points to remember

- **Pythagoras' theorem** can be written as a formula, $a^2 + b^2 = c^2$, where a and b are the lengths of the two shorter sides of a right-angled triangle and c is the length of the hypotenuse.

- If you know the lengths of any two sides of a right-angled triangle, use Pythagoras' theorem to find the length of the third side.

Example

Find length z.

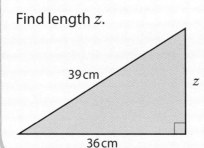

Using Pythagoras' theorem:

$$36^2 + z^2 = 39^2$$
$$1296 + z^2 = 1521$$
$$z^2 = 1521 - 1296 = 225$$
$$z = \sqrt{225} = 15\,\text{cm}$$

You need a calculator.

1. Calculate the length of the unknown side in each of these right-angled triangles. Give your answers to 3 significant figures.

   a
   5 cm, 7 cm, a

   b
   14 cm, 12 cm, b

   c
   7.2 cm, 9.8 cm, c

2. The diagram shows a ladder leaning against a vertical wall. The foot of the ladder is on horizontal ground.

   The length of the ladder is 5 m.
   The foot of the ladder is 3.6 m from the wall.

   Work out how far up the wall the ladder reaches.
   Give your answer correct to 3 significant figures.

   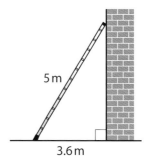

3. Calculate the area of an equilateral triangle whose side length is 10 cm.
   Give your answer to one decimal place.
   Hint: Draw the perpendicular height of the triangle.

TASK 3: Triangles

Example

Is angle x an obtuse angle, an acute angle or a right angle?

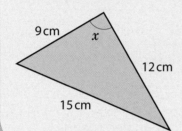

The two shorter sides are 9 and 12.
The sum of their squares is:

$9^2 + 12^2 = 81 + 144 = 225$

The longest side is 15.
$15^2 = 225$ so angle x is a right angle.

Use your calculator. Remember to show your working.

1. For each triangle A to F, state whether it is right-angled, acute-angled or obtuse-angled. Use Pythagoras' theorem to help you to decide.

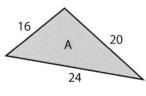

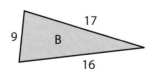

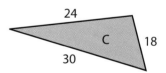

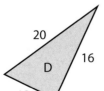

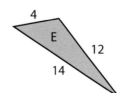

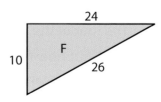

2. Could you construct an isosceles triangle with a base of 9 cm and two equal sides of 5 cm? Explain your answer.

TASK 4: Spirals

You need squared paper, a pair of compasses, a ruler and a pencil.

1. Another type of spiral is the **Fibonacci spiral**. Follow these instructions to draw your own.

   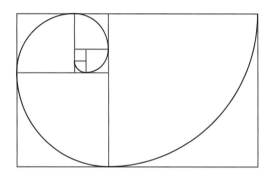

   ▣ In the centre of your squared paper, draw two identical small squares, one on top of the other, each with side length 1 cm.

   ▣ Add a square with side length 2 cm to the right of the first two squares.

   ▣ Add a square of side length 3 cm above the previous squares.

   ▣ Add a square of side length 5 cm to the left of the previous squares.

   ▣ Keep adding larger squares to make the pattern of red squares shown in the diagram.

   ▣ Now draw quarter circles inside each of the squares, as shown in black in the diagram.

   The black curve is called the **Fibonacci spiral**.

2. a The first three squares that you drew had side lengths 1 cm, 1 cm, 2 cm.

   Write the lengths of the sides of the next eight squares in the spiral sequence.

   You should find that these are the **Fibonacci numbers**, which are generated by adding the previous two numbers to get the next term.

   b Calculate the length of the diagonal of each of the eight squares you listed in part a.

TASK 5: Using the trigonometric ratios

Example

Find the length b.

Sketch the triangle.

Label the sides hypotenuse, opposite and adjacent.

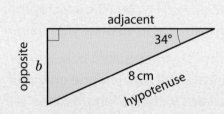

Write down the ratio.

$$\sin \theta = \frac{\text{opposite}}{\text{hypotenuse}}$$

Substitute values you know into the equation.

$$\sin 34° = \frac{b}{8}$$

Calculate sin of the angle.

$$0.559 = \frac{b}{8}$$

Solve the equation.

$$b = 4.47 \text{ cm (to 3 s.f.)}$$

You need a calculator. Give your answers correct to 3 significant figures. Remember to sketch the diagram and to show all your working.

(1) Use the tangent ratio to find the lengths marked with a letter.

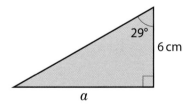

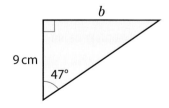

(2) Use the sine ratio to find the lengths marked with a letter.

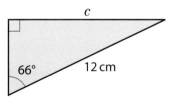

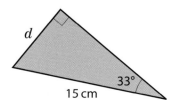

3 Use the cosine ratio to find the missing lengths.

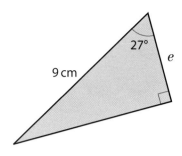

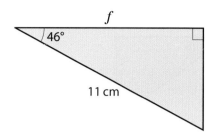

TASK 6: Choosing between sine, cosine and tangent

 Points to remember

⊙ Choose the correct ratio to use to solve each problem.

$$\sin x = \frac{\text{opposite}}{\text{hypotenuse}} \qquad \cos x = \frac{\text{adjacent}}{\text{hypotenuse}} \qquad \tan x = \frac{\text{opposite}}{\text{adjacent}}$$

⊙ **To find an unknown side** of a right-angled triangle:
   – given an angle and one side, choose the ratio that refers to the given and unknown sides;
   – given two sides, use Pythagoras' theorem to calculate the third side.

Example

Find length x.

Sketch the triangle.

Label the sides.

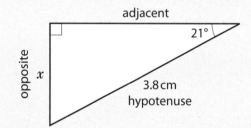

We want to find the opposite side. We know the hypotenuse, so use the sine ratio.

Write down the sine ratio. $\sin = \dfrac{\text{opp}}{\text{hyp}}$

Substitute values you know. $\sin 21° = \dfrac{x}{3.8}$

Calculate the sine of 21°. $0.358 = \dfrac{x}{3.8}$

Solve the equation. $x = 1.36\text{ cm}$ (to 3 s.f.)

You need a calculator.
Remember to sketch the diagram and to show all your working.

1 Find each length marked with a letter.
Give your answers correct to 3 significant figures.

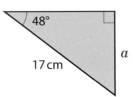 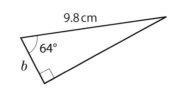 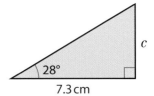

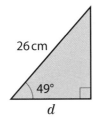 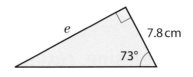 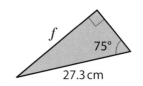

TASK 7: Finding unknown angles

 Points to remember

⊙ **To find an unknown angle** of a right-angled triangle:

- given two sides, choose the ratio that refers to the two sides relative to the unknown angle;

- given the right angle and one other angle, use the angle sum of a triangle to find the third angle.

Example

Find angle b.

Sketch the triangle.

Label the sides.

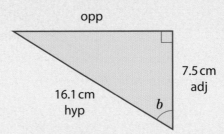

You need to find the angle b.
You know the adjacent side and
the hypotenuse, so use the cosine ratio.

Write down the cosine ratio.

$$\cos = \frac{\text{adj}}{\text{hyp}}$$

Substitute values you know.

$$\cos b = \frac{7.5}{16.1} = 0.4658\ldots$$

Use your calculator to find $\cos^{-1} 0.4658\ldots$
which is $62.237\ldots°$

$$b = 62.237\ldots°$$
$$b = 62.2° \text{ (to 1 d.p.)}$$

You need a calculator.
Remember to sketch the diagram and to show all your working.

1 Find each angle marked with a letter.
Give your answers correct to 1 decimal place.

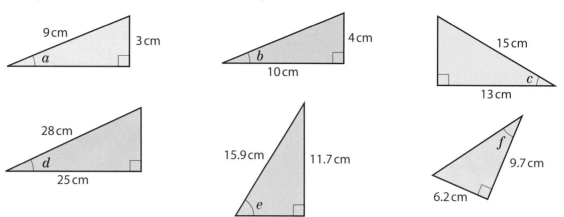

TASK 8: Using trigonometry to solve problems

Points to remember

⊙ Draw a sketch of the triangle in the problem. Mark on the sketch all the known sides and angles, including the units. Label the unknown side or angle with a letter, such as x.

⊙ Label the sides in relation to the given or unknown angle: **opp**osite, **adj**acent, **hyp**otenuse.

⊙ Decide and write down the trigonometric ratio that you need to use to solve the problem. Substitute values you know and solve the equation.

⊙ Give your answer to a suitable degree of accuracy (usually three significant figures for lengths and one decimal place for angles).

Example

Use **trigonometry** to find angles and lengths in right-angled triangles.

The side opposite the right angle is the hypotenuse (hyp).
The side opposite the angle marked x is the opposite side (opp).
The side next to this angle is the adjacent side (adj).

$$\sin x = \frac{\text{opp}}{\text{hyp}} \qquad \cos x = \frac{\text{adj}}{\text{hyp}} \qquad \tan x = \frac{\text{opp}}{\text{adj}}$$

Use **Pythagoras' theorem** to find the length of the third side of a right-angled triangle when the lengths of the other two sides are known.

$$a^2 + b^2 = c^2,$$

where c is the length of the hypotenuse,

and a and b are the lengths of the two shorter sides.

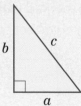

You need a calculator.

Make a sketch of the triangle in each problem and remember to show your working.

Give all your answers correct to 3 significant figures.

1. Find each length marked with a letter.

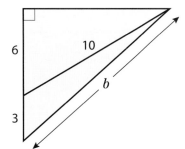

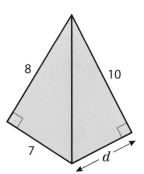

2. Find each length marked with a letter.

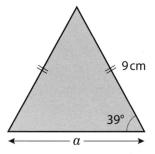

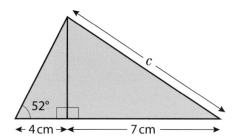

3. A ferry leaves port to travel to an island on a bearing of 050°.

   It travels 80 km to reach the island.

   Draw a sketch of the ferry's journey.

   a How far north of the port is the island?

   b How far east of the port is the island?

Using algebra

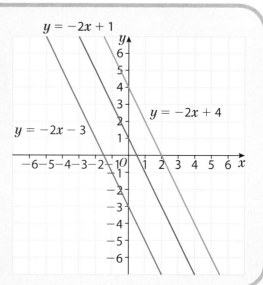

TASK 1: Properties of linear graphs

Points to remember

⊙ The **normal form** of a linear equation is $y = ax + b$.

⊙ The straight line graph $y = ax + b$ has **gradient** a and **intercept** on the y-axis at $(0, b)$.

⊙ The graph of the **inverse** of a linear function is a reflection in the line $y = x$.

Example

This diagram shows the lines with equations:

$$y = -2x - 3 \qquad y = -2x + 1 \qquad y = -2x + 4$$

The **intercept on the y-axis** is the value of y when $x = 0$.

The intercepts on the y-axis for the three lines are:
$-3, +1$ and $+4$

The slope of a line is called its **gradient**.

The gradient of the line $y = -2x + 1$ is **-2**.

As the lines have the same gradient of -2, they are **parallel**.

You need a copy of **A6.4 Resource sheet 1.1** for sketching the graphs.
Use a new grid for each sketch of a graph, and label each line with its equation.

1. Write the gradient and intercept on the y-axis for the graph of each equation.
   Then sketch the graph.

   a $y = -3x - 2$ b $y = 5x - 7$ c $y = -9x + 14$

2. Rearrange each equation in its normal form.
   Write the gradient and intercept on the y-axis for the graph of each equation.
   Then sketch the graph.

   a $y - 4x = 3$ b $5x - y + 3 = 0$ c $2y - 8x = 20$

3. On the same axes, sketch the graph of each function and its inverse.

   a $x \rightarrow \boxed{+5} \rightarrow x + 5$ b $x \rightarrow \boxed{\times 4} \rightarrow 4x$ c $x \rightarrow \boxed{\div 3} \rightarrow \dfrac{x}{3}$

TASK 2: Parallel and perpendicular lines

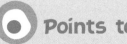 **Points to remember**

- **Parallel lines** have the same gradient.
- Any line parallel to $y = 5x + 2$ is of the form $y = 5x + b$ and has a gradient of 5.
- Any line **perpendicular** to $y = 5x + 2$ is of the form $y = -\frac{x}{5} + b$ and has a gradient of $-\frac{1}{5}$.

Example

Find an equation of the line which passes through the point $(-2, 1)$ and which is parallel to $y = -2x + 5$.

$y = -2x + 5$ has gradient -2.

The gradient of any parallel line is -2.
It has an equation of the form $y = -2x + c$.

$(-2, 1)$ is a point on $y = -2x + c$, so substituting $x = -2$ and $y = 1$ gives $1 = 4 + c$, or $c = -3$.

So an equation of the line is $y = -2x - 3$.

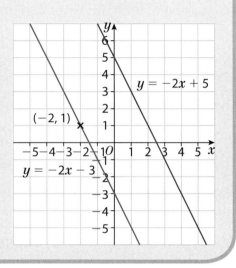

1. a A line is parallel to $y = 2x + 7$. It intersects the y-axis at $(0, -4)$.
       What is its equation?

    b A line is parallel to $y = -7x + 3$. It intersects the y-axis at $(0, 4)$.
       What is its equation?

    c A line passes through $(2, 1)$ and $(4, 7)$. It intersects the y-axis at $(0, 5)$.
       What is its equation?

2. A line has equation $y = 3x - 7$. A line parallel to this line passes through the point $(1, 7)$.
    What is its equation?

3. In each question, you are given the coordinates of four points: **A, B, C** and **D**.
    Decide whether the line segments AB and CD are parallel, perpendicular or neither.

    a **A** is $(2, 2)$; **B** is $(3, 7)$; **C** is $(3, 1)$ and **D** is $(4, 6)$

    b **A** is $(-2, 1)$; **B** is $(-4, 5)$; **C** is $(3, 2)$ and **D** is $(7, 4)$

TASK 3: Generating quadratic graphs with ICT

  Points to remember

⊙ A **quadratic equation** is one in which the highest power of x is x^2.

⊙ The **normal form** of a quadratic equation is $y = ax^2 + bx + c$.

⊙ The graph of a quadratic equation is a symmetrical U-shaped curve.
When a is negative the U-shaped curve is reflected in the x-axis.

⊙ A quadratic graph may cut or touch the x-axis at two points, one point
or not at all.

⊙ The **turning point** shows the **minimum or maximum** value of y for
the equation.

You need a copy of **A6.4 Resource sheet 3.1**.
Use a new grid for each sketch of a graph, and label each line with its equation.

1 Describe the shape of any quadratic graph.

2 Which of the graphs below are quadratic graphs?

a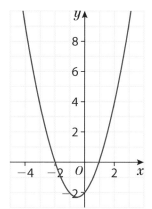

b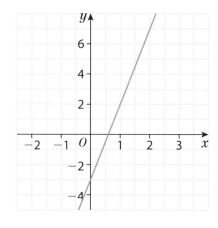

c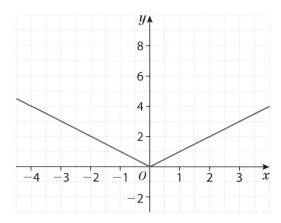

d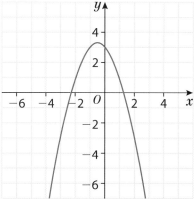

3 Sketch each of these graphs.

a $y = x^2 + 4$ b $y = -x^2 + 3$

TASK 4: Generating cubic graphs with ICT

Points to remember

⊙ A **cubic equation** is one in which the highest power of x is x^3.

⊙ The normal form of a cubic equation is $y = ax^3 + bx^2 + cx + d$.

⊙ The graph of a cubic function is an S-shaped curve.

⊙ A cubic graph may cut or touch the x-axis at three points or one point.

⊙ A cubic graph has two turning points or no turning point.

You will need **A6.4 Resource sheet 1.1**.

(1) Describe the shape of any cubic graph.

(2) Which of the graphs below are cubic graphs?

a
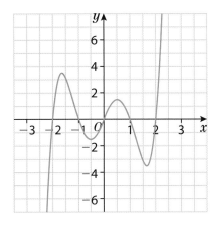

b
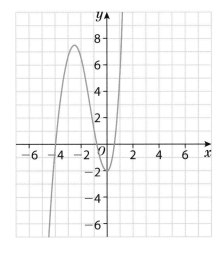

c
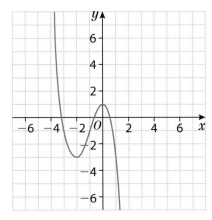

d
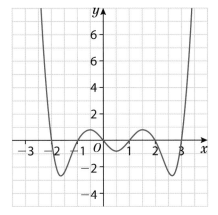

(3) Sketch each of these graphs on a new grid.

  a $y = x^3 - 2$ b $y = -x^3 + 1$

TASK 5: Drawing graphs

 Points to remember

- To draw the graph of a **linear function**, you need only plot the coordinates of three points.
- To draw the graph of a **quadratic function**, you need to plot enough points to be able to draw a smooth curve.

You need graph paper.

1 **a** Copy and complete this table of values for the equation $y = x^2 + 5$.

x	−3	−2	−1	0	1	2	3
y							

b Draw the graph of $y = x^2 + 5$.

2 **a** Copy and complete this table of values for the equation $y = -x^2 + 1$.

x	−3	−2	−1	0	1	2	3
y							

b Draw the graph of $y = -x^2 + 1$.

TASK 6: Using graphs to help solve equations

 Points to remember

- Equations can be represented as **graphs**.
- You can read **integer solutions** to equations and **first estimates** directly from graphs.
- Use **trial and improvement** to find solutions of equations to a given number of decimal places.
- You can use graphs as a visual check of algebraic solutions to equations.

1 Solve these pairs of simultaneous equations by drawing their graphs.

a $2x + 3y = 16$
$3x - 4y = 7$

b $3x + 8y = 10$
$2x + 7y = 5$

Solve these quadratic equations using the method of trial and improvement.
Sketch a graph to get a first estimate for each solution.

a $2x^2 + 4x - 5 = 0$ b $x^2 + 3x - 7 = 0$

TASK 7: Interpreting graphs

◉ Points to remember

⊙ When you interpret a **'real-life' graph**:
  – look at the labels and decide what is represented on each axis;
  – work out the scale on each axis;
  – look at the shape of the graph and think about what happens to one
    variable as the other variable increases.

1   The graph shows the conversion between pounds sterling and euros in 2008.

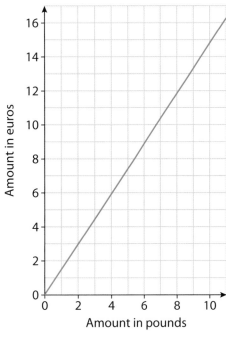

a   Estimate from the graph how many euros were equivalent to £10.

b   Alex saved £300 to take with him on holiday.
    Estimate how many euros he could buy for this.

c   Alex bought a present for his brother costing 10 euros.
    How many pounds was this?

d   Alex came home with 50 euros.
    About how many pounds did he get for this?

e   Find out whether banks buy and sell euros at the same rate.

(2) The graph shows Karim's journey with his friend Jamal.

Karim set off from home at 11 am.
He met Jamal at Burton bus stop.
They just managed to catch the bus to Allerton.
They got off the bus and had lunch at a café.
They then went for a walk.
They caught a bus back to Burton.
Karim then walked home.

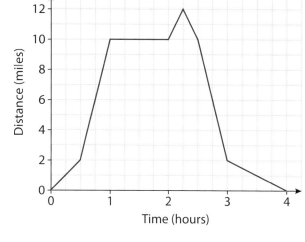

a Use the graph to tell a different story of your own.

b Write some questions to a friend about the graph.

TASK 8: Investigations

 Points to remember

⊙ Read through the problem and decide what mathematics you will use.

⊙ Define any variables.

⊙ Use mathematics to model the problem, e.g. draw a diagram, write an equation or draw a graph.

⊙ Solve the problem and interpret the solution in terms of the original investigation.

⊙ Justify or prove the results.

(1) Look at these towers of bricks.

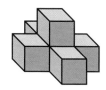 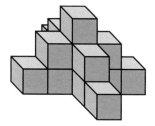

a How many bricks are in each tower?

b How many bricks will be in the fourth tower?

c How many bricks will be in the tenth tower?

d How many bricks will be in the nth tower? Explain how you know.

Probability 2

TASK 1: Tree diagrams 1

> **◉ Points to remember**
>
> - **Mutually exclusive** outcomes of an event or of combined events cannot occur at the same time.
> - If **A** and **B** are two mutually exclusive outcomes of an event then:
>   P(**A** or **B**) = P(**A**) + P(**B**)
> - You can use **tree diagrams** to represent mutually exclusive outcomes of combined events and their probabilities.

1. Avi buys an ice cream from a shop that sells two flavours of ice cream, chocolate (**C**) and vanilla (**V**).

    Ben buys an ice cream from a kiosk that sells three flavours of ice cream, chocolate (**C**), vanilla (**V**) and strawberry (**S**).

    Avi and Ben choose the flavour of their ice creams at random.

    a Copy and complete this tree diagram to show all the possible choices of flavours that Avi and Ben can make.

    | Avi | Ben | Possible choices of flavour |

    C

    b Use the tree diagram to work out the probability that Avi and Ben buy:
      i two chocolate ice creams
      ii two ice creams with the same flavour
      iii at least one chocolate ice cream
      iv at least one strawberry ice cream **or** at least one vanilla ice cream

TASK 2: Tree diagrams 2

 Points to remember

- ⊙ The probabilities of the outcomes of each event can be written on the branches of a tree diagram.
- ⊙ Each set of branches should include all the mutually exclusive outcomes of the event.
- ⊙ The sum of the probabilities on each set of branches is 1.
- ⊙ Use the probabilities on the branches to work out the probabilities of combined outcomes.
- ⊙ The sum of the probabilities of all the mutually exclusive combined outcomes is 1.

1. The tree diagram represents a network of roads.

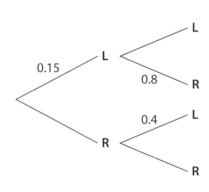

The probability of a vehicle travelling along some of the routes in the network is shown on the branches.

For example, the probability of a vehicle turning left at the first junction is 0.15.

a Copy the tree diagram.
Complete the probabilities on the branches.

b 100 vehicles pass through the network.
On average, how many vehicles take these routes?
  i **L** and **L**   ii **L** and **R**   iii **R** and **L**   iv **R** and **R**

c Work out these probabilities.
  i P(**L** and **L** or **R** and **R**)   ii P(**L** and **R** or **R** and **L**)

2 Traffic travels through this network of roads.

At each junction the probability that traffic turns in the direction of the arrows is shown.

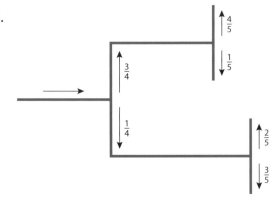

a Copy and complete this tree diagram to represent the network.

b 100 vehicles enter the network. On average, how many vehicles take these routes through the network?

   i   **L** and **L**

  ii   **L** and **R**

 iii   **R** and **L**

 iv   **R** and **R**

c Work out these probabilities.

   i   P(**L** and **L**)   ii   P(**L** and **R**)   iii   P(**R** and **L**)   iv   P(**R** and **R**)

d Vehicles going either **L** and **R** or **R** and **L** go to the city centre car park.

Work out the probability that a car goes to the city centre car park.

TASK 3: Tree diagrams 3

 Points to remember

⊙ When one event happening does not affect the probability of another event happening, the events are independent.

⊙ The probabilities of the outcomes of combined independent events can be worked out from a tree diagram.

⊙ Multiply the probabilities on the branches that represent each combined outcome, so when A and B are the outcomes of two independent events:

   P(**A** and **B**) = P(**A**) × P(**B**)

1 A bag contains 7 red balls (**R**) and 13 blue balls (**B**).

A ball is taken at random from the bag and its colour is recorded. The ball is replaced. A second ball is taken at random from the bag and its colour recorded.

a Copy and complete this tree diagram to show all the possible outcomes of these two events. Write the probabilities of each outcome on the branches.

First pick	Second pick	Combined outcome	Probabilities

$$\frac{7}{20} \qquad R \qquad R \text{ and } R \qquad \frac{7}{20} \times \frac{7}{20} = \frac{49}{400}$$

R

$\frac{7}{20}$

$\frac{7}{20}$

B

b Work out the probability that:
  i the balls have the same colour
  ii the balls have a different colour

2 Two shops sell ice cream of different flavours.
The probabilities of each different flavour for each shop are shown in the table.

Flavour	Vanilla (V)	Chocolate (C)	Strawberry (S)
Shop A	$\frac{1}{2}$	$\frac{1}{4}$	$\frac{1}{4}$
Shop B	$\frac{1}{2}$	$\frac{2}{5}$	$\frac{1}{10}$

A customer, chosen at random, buys an ice cream from shop A.
A different customer, chosen at random, buys an ice cream from shop B.

a Copy and complete this tree diagram together with a list of all the possible choices of ice cream the two customers can buy.

Write the probabilities of each outcome on the branches of the diagram.

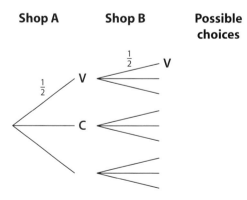

b Work out the probability that:
  i both customers buy a vanilla ice cream
  ii at least one customer buys a vanilla ice cream
  iii both customers by the same flavour ice cream
  iv both customers buy a different flavour ice cream

TASK 4: Relative frequency and probability

> ## Points to remember
> ⊙ You can test whether or not a trial is fair by comparing the **relative frequency** of outcomes from the trial with the **theoretical probability** of the outcomes, provided that the number of trials is large.

You need a coin and some graph paper.

①　A coin is flipped three times.

　　a　Copy and complete this tree diagram to show the outcomes of heads or not heads for three flips of the coin.

　　b　Use the tree diagram to work out the probability of getting at least one head in three flips of the coin. Write this probability as a decimal to 3 decimal places.

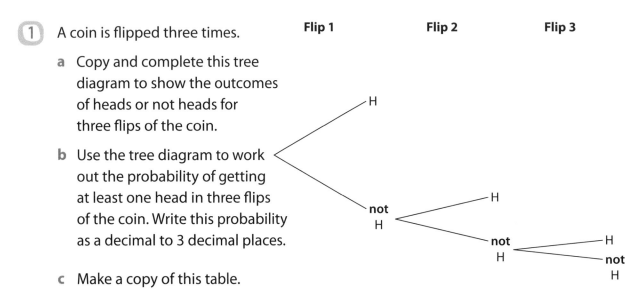

Flip 1　　　　**Flip 2**　　　　**Flip 3**

　　c　Make a copy of this table.

Number of trials	Getting at least one head in 3 flips Tally	Cumulative frequency	Relative frequency
10			
20			
30			
40			
50			

　　d　Flip your coin up to three times.
　　　　Record in the tally column of the table whether or not you get a head.
　　　　Repeat the trial 50 times.
　　　　Now complete the cumulative frequency and relative frequency columns of your table.

　　e　Draw a relative frequency graph to show the relative frequency of getting a head in up to three flips of a coin. Plot the relative frequency for every 10 trials.

　　f　Describe how the relative frequency of getting a head in up to three flips of a coin changes as the number of trials increases.

Using and applying maths

TASK 1: The history of π

 Points to remember

⊙ People from many different cultures have contributed to work on π throughout the ages.

⊙ The Internet is a useful source of information about mathematics and its history but it is important to find the best website.

⊙ It is often necessary to narrow down an Internet search so that it results in **a** less information, and **b** more relevant information.

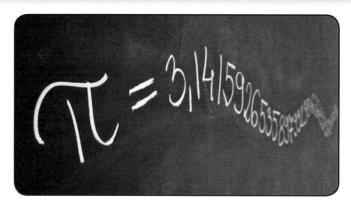

During your research on π and its history you may have looked at one or both of these websites:

www.joyofpi.com/pilinks.html and **wasi.org/PI/pi_club.html**

Write a short article of four or five paragraphs based on the notes you have made during your research. Assume that your article will be published in a magazine for Key Stage 3 pupils.

Make sure that you give your article a suitable title.

TASK 2: Limits of sequences

1 A sequence is described like this.

The first term is A.
The term-to-term rule to find the next term of the sequence is 'add B'.

If $A = 5$, and $B = 3$, the sequence is 5, 8, 11, 14, 17, …

Find two pairs of possible values for A and B that would make:

a all the numbers in the sequence even;

b all the numbers in the sequence odd;

c all the numbers in the sequence multiples of 3;

d all the numbers in the sequence end in the same digit;

e exactly nine two-digit numbers in the sequence;

f every other number in the sequence a whole number;

g every fourth number in the sequence a whole number;

h every fourth number in the sequence a multiple of 5.

TASK 3: Investigating paper sizes

Points to remember

- A **ratio** compares two or more quantities.
- Ratios are simplified like fractions.
- The ratio $a:b$ can be stated in the form of the **unitary ratio** $1:\dfrac{b}{a}$.
- To compare ratios, write them as unitary ratios.
- Corresponding sides of similar shapes are in the same ratio.

You need some squared paper.

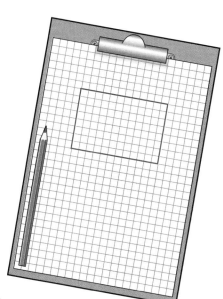

1. Draw rectangle A with length 120 mm and width 80 mm.
   Write the dimensions on the rectangle.

   a Halve the rectangle parallel to the shorter side
      to get rectangle B.
      Write its dimensions on the rectangle.

   b Halve the second rectangle parallel to its
      shorter side to get rectangle C.
      Write its dimensions on the rectangle.

   c Halve the third rectangle parallel to its
      shorter side to get rectangle D.
      Write its dimensions on the rectangle.

   d You should now have four rectangles:
      A, B, C and D.
      For each rectangle, divide its length by its width.
      What do you notice?

2. Repeat question 1 starting with a rectangle of a different size.
   The width must be more than half the length.
   What do you notice this time? Does the same thing happen?

3. Find a starting rectangle A for which the length divided by the width is the same for
   all four rectangles A, B, C and D.

TASK 4: Proof

① Harry says that $n^2 + 3n + 1$ is a prime number for all integer values of n.

Harry is wrong.
Explain why.

② Hannah says:

> The cube of any number is always bigger than the square of the same number.

Is Hannah correct?
Write **Yes** or **No**.
Explain your reasoning.

③ Explain why the difference between two multiples of 4 is also a multiple of 4.

④ If b is an even number, prove that

$$(b + 1)(b - 1)$$

is an odd number.

TASK 5: Maths in our lives

⊙ Points to remember

- ⊙ The use of maths is widespread in everyday life, from children's toys and games, to driving and shopping, and practical tasks around the home or garden.
- ⊙ Many different occupations use maths in some way, sometimes in ways that are not immediately obvious.

1 In the lesson, you looked at the ways in which maths is used in everyday life and at work. You produced a presentation on three different occupations that make use of maths.

Scientist   Carpenter   Chef

Think about your presentation and how you went about it.

a Which occupations did you choose?

b For each occupation, explain briefly how maths is used in it.

c Were these the best occupations to choose? Why or why not?

d How satisfied were you with the quality of your presentation? Give your reasons.

e Describe two different ways in which you would improve your presentation if you were doing it again.

Revision unit 1

TASK 1: Fractions and percentages

 Points to remember

- To **add or subtract mixed numbers**, deal with whole numbers first.
- To **multiply fractions**, cancel, then multiply the numerators and multiply the denominators.
- To **divide fractions** turn the divisor upside down and multiply by it.
- When you **multiply or divide mixed numbers**, first convert them to improper fractions.
- Use the **unitary method** or **decimal multipliers** to work out percentage changes.

Do question 1 **without using a calculator**. For questions 2, 3 and 4, you may **use a calculator**.

1 *2003 level 6*

    a How many quarters are there in $4\frac{1}{2}$?   **b** How many tenths are there in $3\frac{3}{5}$?

    c Work out $3\frac{3}{5} \div \frac{3}{10}$. Show your working.

2 *1996 KS2 level 6*

    a Write a fraction which is greater than 0.7 and less than 0.71.

    b Write a decimal which is greater than $\frac{4}{7}$ and less than $\frac{5}{7}$.

3 *2001 level 6*

The population of the world is approximately 6200 million people.
It is increasing by approximately 93 million people each year.

    a Use this information to calculate the percentage increase in the population over a year. Show your working.

    b Mike says:

> An increase of 93 million people each year is more than 170 people each minute.

Show that he is correct.

4 *1998 level 6*

The table shows the land area of each of the world's continents.

a Which continent is approximately 12% of the world's land area?

b What percentage of the world's land area is Antarctica? Show your working.

c About 30% of the world's area is land. The rest is water. The amount of land in the world is about 150 million km².

Work out the approximate total area (land and water) of the world. Show your working.

Continent	Land area (in 1000 km²)
Africa	30 264
Antarctica	13 209
Asia	44 250
Europe	9 907
North America	24 398
Oceania	8 534
South America	17 793
World	148 355

TASK 2: Ratio and proportion

Points to remember

⊙ Two quantities a and b are **directly proportional** if their ratio $a:b$ stays the same as the quantities increase or decrease, so:

$\frac{a}{b} = k$, where k is constant.

⊙ Use the **unitary method** to solve direct proportion problems by reducing the value of one of the variables to 1.

⊙ When a quantity is divided into two parts in the **ratio** $a:b$, the parts are $\frac{a}{a+b}$ and $\frac{b}{a+b}$ of the whole quantity.

1 *1999 level 6*

a Use £1 = 9.6 Swiss francs to work out how much 45p is in Swiss francs.
Show your working.

b Use 240 Japanese yen = £1 to work out how much 408 yen is in pounds.
Show your working.

c Use £1 = 9.6 Swiss francs and £1 = 240 Japanese yen to work out how much 1 Swiss franc is in Japanese yen.
Show your working.

(2) *GCSE 2540 May 2008*

Pancakes
Ingredients to make 8 pancakes

300 ml milk
1 egg
120 g flour
5 g butter

a Jacob makes 24 pancakes.
Work out how much milk he needs.

b Cathie makes 12 pancakes.
Work out how much flour she needs.

(3) *1999 KS2 level 6*

The diagram shows a shaded triangle inside a larger triangle.

The area of the shaded triangle is 52 cm². The area of the shaded triangle is $\frac{4}{9}$ of the area of the larger triangle.

Calculate the area of the larger triangle.

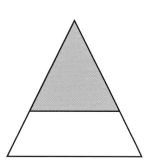

(4) *1996 level 6*

Emlyn is doing a project on world population.
He has found some data about the population of the regions of the world in 1950 and 1990.

Regions of the world	Population (in millions) in 1950	Population (in millions) in 1990
Africa	222	642
Asia	1558	3402
Europe	393	498
Latin America	166	448
North America	166	276
Oceania	13	26
World	2518	5292

a In 1990, for every person who lived in North America how many people lived in Asia? Show your working.

b For every person who lived in Africa in 1950 how many people lived in Africa in 1990? Show your working

c Emlyn thinks that from 1950 to 1990 the population of Oceania went up by 100%. Is Emlyn right? Write **Yes** or **No** or **Cannot tell**. Explain your answer.

TASK 3: Expressions and equations

Points to remember

- In an algebraic **expression**, the letters stand for numbers.
- To find the value of an algebraic expression, substitute a value for each of the variables.
- **A linear equation**, such as $3x - 5 = 2x$, has a unique solution, i.e. $x = 5$.
- To expand a bracket, multiply every term inside the bracket by the number outside, e.g. $5(3x + 4) = 15x + 20$.
- To expand a pair of brackets, use a multiplication grid, or use FOIL, e.g. $(x + 3)(x + 2) = x^2 + 2x + 3x + 6 = x^2 + 5x + 6$.

(1) *GCSE 1388 March 2005*

Expand and simplify:

$(x - 9)(x + 4)$

(2) *2006 level 7*

Solve this equation:

$3y + 14 = 5y + 1$

(3) *GCSE 1388 March 2004*

$P = Q^2 - 2Q$

Find the value of P when $Q = -3$.

(4) *GCSE 1388 March 2005*

The number of diagonals, D, of a polygon with n sides is given by this formula.

A polygon has 20 sides.
Work out the number of diagonals of this polygon.

$$D = \frac{n^2 - 3n}{2}$$

(5) *GCSE 1388 June 2004*

The lengths, in cm, of the sides of the triangle are $3(x - 3)$, $4x - 1$ and $2x + 5$.

a Write down, in terms of x, an expression for the perimeter of the triangle.

b The perimeter of the triangle is 49 cm.
Work out the value of x.

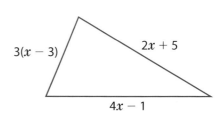

TASK 4: Angles and triangles

◉ Points to remember

- **Pythagoras' theorem** applies only to right-angled triangles.

- The **hypotenuse** is opposite the right-angle and is the longest side. The **opposite** side is opposite the given or unknown angle and the **adjacent** side is next to it.

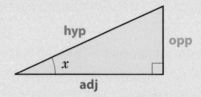

- To solve a right-angled triangle problem, sketch the triangle and mark on it all the known sides and angles, including the units. Label the unknown side or angle, e.g. with x.

- Label the sides in relation to the given or unknown angle: **opp**osite, **adj**acent, **hyp**otenuse.

- $\sin x = \dfrac{\text{opp}}{\text{hyp}}$, $\cos x = \dfrac{\text{adj}}{\text{hyp}}$, $\tan x = \dfrac{\text{opp}}{\text{adj}}$

- Decide and write down the trigonometric ratio that you need to use. Substitute values you know and solve the equation.

- Give your answer to a suitable degree of accuracy (3 s.f. for lengths and 1 d.p. for angles).

① *2001 level 7*

   a Calculate the length of the unknown side of this right-angled triangle.

     Show your working.

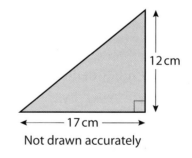

12 cm

17 cm

Not drawn accurately

   b Calculate the length of the unknown side of this right-angled triangle.

     Show your working.

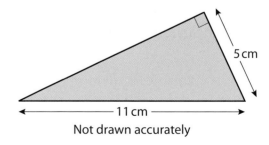

5 cm

11 cm

Not drawn accurately

2 *2006 level 6*

Look at the diagram, made from
four straight lines.
The lines marked with arrows
are parallel.

Work out the sizes of the angles
marked with letters.

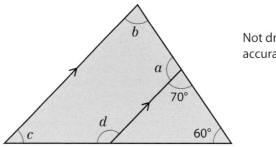

Not drawn
accurately

3 *2005 level 7*

ABCD is a parallelogram.

Work out the sizes of angles *h* and *j*.
Give reasons for your answers.

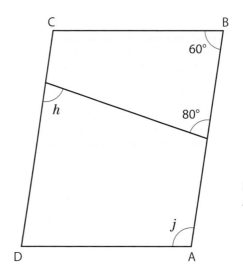

Not drawn
accurately

4 *GCSE 1388 March 2004*

The diagram shows triangle ABC.

Angle ABC = 90°
Angle ACB = 24°
AC = 6.2 cm

Calculate the length of BC.
Give your answer correct to 3 significant figures.

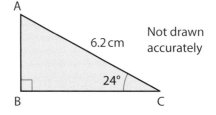

Not drawn
accurately

5 *GCSE 1387 June 2003*

The diagram shows triangle ABC.

BC = 8.5 cm
Angle ABC = 90°
Angle ACB = 38°

Work out the length of AB.
Give your answer correct to 3 significant figures.

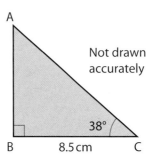

Not drawn
accurately

TASK 5: Probability

 Points to remember

- **Mutually exclusive outcomes** cannot occur at the same time. If **A** and **B** are mutually exclusive, then:

  P(**A** or **B**) = P(**A**) + P(**B**)

- Two events are **independent** if one event occurring does not affect the probability of the other event occurring.

- Use **two-way tables** and **tree diagrams** to identify the possible outcomes of two independent events and work out their probabilities.

- If **A** is an outcome of one event and **B** is an outcome of an independent event, then:

  P(**A** and **B**) = P(**A**) × P(**B**)

(1) Heather rolls a fair dice and flips a fair coin at the same time.

a Explain why rolling the dice and flipping the coin are independent events.

b Heather completes this two-way table. Copy and complete Heather's table.

c Heather says that the probability of obtaining a head and a 6 is $\frac{1}{4}$. Explain why she is wrong.

| | Coin | |
	Head	Tail
6	**H** and **6**	
not 6		

Dice

d Copy and complete this tree diagram to show the same outcomes as Heather shows in the table.

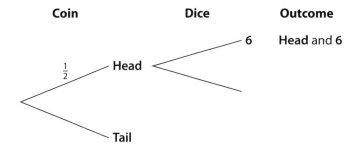

e Use the tree diagram to show that the probability of flipping a head and rolling a 6 is $\frac{1}{12}$.

f Work out the probability that Heather flips a tail and does not roll a 6. Show your working.

(2) *1995 level 6*

Alun has these two spinners.

Alun spins both spinners and then adds up the numbers to get a total.

He draws a two-way table to find all the possible totals.

Copy and complete Alun's table.

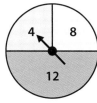
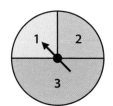

Spinner A   Spinner B

Spinner A

		4	8	12
Spinner B	1	5		
	2			
	3			

(3) Alun has these two spinners.

Alun spins both spinners and then adds up the numbers to get a total.

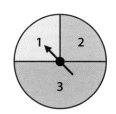

Spinner A   Spinner B

a The probabilities that the spinners land on each number are shown in these tables.

Spinner A	
Number	**Probability**
4	$\frac{1}{4}$
8	$\frac{1}{4}$
12	$\frac{1}{2}$

Spinner B	
Number	**Probability**
1	$\frac{1}{4}$
2	$\frac{1}{4}$
3	$\frac{1}{2}$

Copy and complete this tree diagram to show each possible total.

b Use your tree diagram to work out the probability of getting a total score of:

i 5   ii 10   iii 15

Show your working.

Spinner A	Spinner B	Outcomes	Total
	1	4 and 1	5

Revision unit 2

TASK 1: Decimals

 Points to remember

- A number rounded to **one significant figure** has only one non-zero digit.
- A number in **standard form** is of the form: $A \times 10^n$, where $1 \leqslant A < 10$ and n is an integer.
- You can estimate answers by rounding numbers to one significant figure or another sensible approximation.
- In an exact calculation, round the final answer, not the intermediate steps.
- Measurements may be inaccurate by up to half a unit in either direction.

Do questions 1–4 **without your calculator**. Show your working.

1 *1999 level 6*

Write three decimals, each greater than 1, which add together to make 0.01.

$$\ldots + \ldots + \ldots = 0.01$$

2 *GCSE 1387 November 2007*

   a Work out £3.75 $\times$ 24.

   b Divide £135 by 20.

3 *GCSE 1387 November 2007*

   a Write 7900 in standard form.

   b Write 0.000 35 in standard form.

4 *GCSE 1387 November 2006*

Estimate the value of $\dfrac{21 \times 3.86}{0.207}$.

You may **use a calculator** for questions 5 and 6.

5 *GCSE 1387 June 2007*

   a Use your calculator to work out the value of $\sqrt{20.25} + 1.65^2$.
Write down all the figures on your calculator display.

   b Write your answer to part **a** correct to 1 decimal place.

6 *1996 level 7*

Gary makes a sphere with diameter 3.6 cm using modelling clay.

The volume of a sphere is $\dfrac{\pi d^3}{6}$, where d is the diameter.

   a Work out the volume of clay in the sphere.
Give your answer to a sensible degree of accuracy.

   b Gary uses some more clay to make this shape.

The volume of the shape is $\frac{1}{4}\pi^2(a + b)(b - a)^2$.

Gary makes $a = 4.5$ cm and $b = 7.5$ cm.
Work out the volume of clay used.
Show your working.

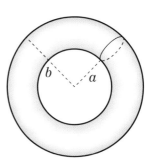

   c The surface area of the shape is $\pi^2(b^2 - a^2)$.
Work out the surface area of the shape.

TASK 2: Sequences and graphs

⦿ Points to remember

⊙ The **first difference** between consecutive terms of a **linear sequence** is constant. For example, in the linear sequence 5, 9, 13, 17, … , the first difference is 4 and the nth term is $4n + 1$.

⊙ The **second difference** between terms of a **quadratic sequence** is constant. For example, in the quadratic sequence 1, 3, 6, 10. … , the second difference is 1 and the nth term is $\frac{1}{2}n(n + 1)$.

⊙ The **normal form** of the equation of a linear graph is $y = ax + b$, where a is the gradient and $(0, b)$ is the intercept on the y-axis.

⊙ Lines parallel to $y = ax + b$ also have gradient a.

(1) *GCSE 1388 March 2004*

   a Here are the first five terms of an arithmetic sequence.

$$-1 \quad 3 \quad 7 \quad 11 \quad 15$$

   Find, in terms of n, an expression for the nth term of this sequence.

   b In another arithmetic sequence the nth term is $8n - 16$.

   John says that there is a number that is in both sequences.
   Explain why John is wrong.

(2) *2005 Mental Test level 7*

What is the gradient of the line with equation $y = 2x + 3$?

(3) Write the gradient, the y-axis intercept and the equation of each of these graphs:

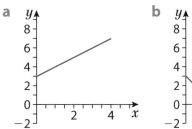 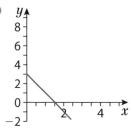 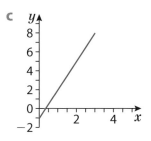 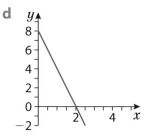

(4) *GCSE 1387 November 2003*

A straight line passes through the point with coordinates (4, 7).
It is parallel to the line with equation $y = 2x + 3$.
Find an equation of the straight line.

TASK 3: Graphs and equations

Points to remember

⊙ When you interpret **graphs of real-life situations**, always check what the axes represent and work out the scales on the axes.

⊙ You can use **trial and improvement** to solve equations methodically.
   – Start with an estimate. Substitute this and use the feedback to improve your next estimate.
   – Carry on until you have the required number of figures in the solution.

(1) *1997 level 7*

A child is having a bath. The simplified graph shows the depth of the water in the bath.

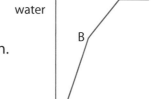

a From A to B both taps are turned full on. What might be happening at point B?

b Which part of the graph shows the child getting into the bath?

c Which part of the graph shows the child getting out of the bath?

(2) The diagrams show three containers filling up with water.
d is the diameter of the surface of the water when the height of the water is h.

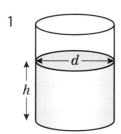

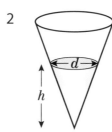

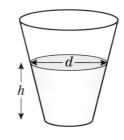

a These graphs each show a relationship between d and h.
Match the graphs with the containers.

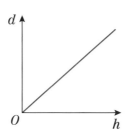

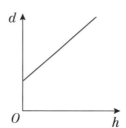

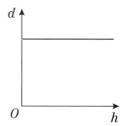

b Water leaks at a constant rate from a hole in the bottom of one of the containers.

This graph shows the relationship between the height of water h and the time t.
Which container is leaking?

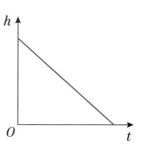

(3) *GCSE 1387 November 2007*

The equation $x^3 - 5x = 60$ has a solution between 4 and 5.
Use a trial and improvement method to find this solution.
Give your answer correct to 1 decimal place. You must show all your working.

TASK 4: 2D and 3D shapes

Points to remember

⊙ When you **enlarge** a shape, measure distances of the vertices from the centre of enlargement. If C is the centre, for corresponding points P' and P on the image and object CP' = scale factor × CP.

⊙ **Volume of prism** = area of cross-section × length

You need some squared paper.

1 *GCSE 1387 June 2004*

Copy the grid and the shaded triangle on squared paper.

Enlarge the shaded triangle by a scale factor 2, centre *O*.

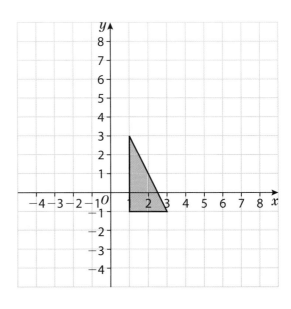

2 *GCSE 1387 June 2007*

Work out the total surface area of the L-shaped prism.

State the units with your answer.

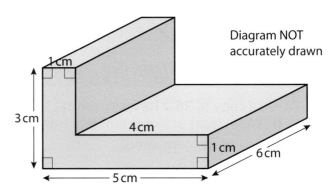

Diagram NOT accurately drawn

3 *GCSE 1388 March 2007*

A solid metal cylinder has a radius of 8 cm and a height of 15 cm.

Calculate the volume of the cylinder. Give your answer to the nearest whole number.

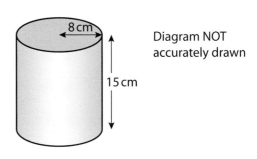

Diagram NOT accurately drawn

4 *GCSE 1387 June 3003*

Here are the plan and front elevation of a prism.

The front elevation shows the cross-section of the prism.

Plan

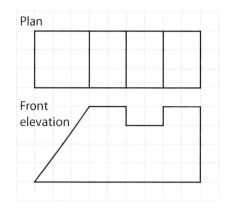

a On squared paper, draw a side elevation of the prism.

b Draw a 3-D sketch of the prism.

Front elevation

TASK 5: Grouped frequency

 Points to remember

⊙ **A line of best fit** represents the best estimate of the relationship between the two variables on a scatter graph. To draw it, draw a straight line so that the points on the scatter graph are balanced on each side of it.

⊙ To draw a **frequency polygon** for a set of grouped data:
  – plot the frequencies (f) against the midpoints of the class intervals (x);
  – join the points with straight lines.

⊙ The **modal class** is the class interval with the greatest frequency.

⊙ To estimate **the mean of a set of grouped data**:
  – for each interval, work out $x \times f$;
  – find the total of the products $x \times f$;
  – divide by the sum of the frequencies f.

You need a copy of **R6.2 Resource sheet 5.3**.

1 *GCSE 1387 June 2007*

The table gives some information about the time taken by a group of 100 students to complete an IQ test.

a Write down the modal class interval.

b Calculate an estimate for the mean time taken by the students.

Show your working.

Time (t seconds)	Frequency	
$60 \leqslant t < 70$	12	
$70 \leqslant t < 80$	22	
$80 \leqslant t < 90$	23	
$90 \leqslant t < 100$	24	
$100 \leqslant t < 110$	19	

2 A survey was carried out to find the time taken for people to do their shopping at two supermarkets.

The results are shown in the table.

Time taken, t (minutes)	Supermarket 1 Frequency	Supermarket 2 Frequency
$0 \leqslant t < 10$	41	23
$10 \leqslant t < 20$	37	48
$20 \leqslant t < 30$	16	21
$30 \leqslant t < 40$	6	8

a This frequency polygon shows the times taken at **Supermarket 1**.

On the frequency polygon on **Resource sheet 5.3**, draw a frequency polygon for Supermarket 2.

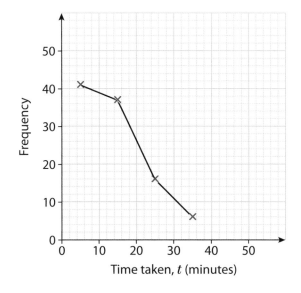

b Copy and complete the table below.

	Measures of average		Measure of spread
	Modal class	Estimate of mean	Estimate of range
Supermarket 1			
Supermarket 2			

Show your working.

c Use the frequency polygons and the completed table to compare the times spent in each supermarket.

The scatter graph shows some information about seven children.
It shows the age of each child and the number of hours sleep each child had last night.

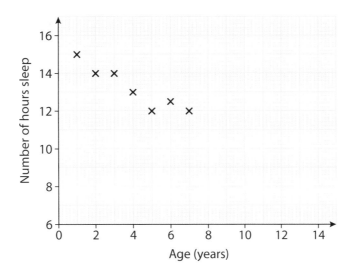

Age (years)

The table shows the ages of four more children and the number of hours sleep each of them had last night.

Age (years)	10	11	12	13
Number of hours sleep	11	10	10.5	9.6

a   On the scatter graph on **Resource sheet 5.3**, plot the information from the table.

b   Describe the correlation between the age, in years, of the children and the number of hours sleep they had last night.

c   Draw a line of best fit on the diagram.

d   Use your line of best fit to estimate the number of hours sleep for an 8-year-old child.